A Summer Cottage Through A Child's Eye

Linda McFarlane Knierim

This book is intended for the readers to enjoy how a little girl's dream became true. Every intention was made not to judge anyone and to keep the book complete as possible with facts from a child's view.

ISBN 13 9781530824571

DEDICATION

To My Mom and Dad

Thank you both for the gifts of Cooking, Love of Flowers,

AND MOST IMPORTANTLY

THE LOVE OF A FAMILY YOU HAVE GIVEN ME…

ACKNOWLEDGEMENT

Through the journey of writing "A Summer Cottage" I have so many to thank. The first one is my husband, Doug, for his love, confidence, and support. He had to put up with me saying over and over, "Do you think everyone will love my summer cottage book? With a half-smile he would often give me, and saying, *"Your summer cottage"*? Thanking my four children Heather, Patrick (Rick), Katie, and Jillian for their confidence by telling me that I could write this story. To Nita, Audrey, and Howard (Benny)--my siblings and to their families, Lynn, Dawne, Nancy, and Kacie for the memories I have been able to share.

Also thank you to other family members and friends who have either shared memories or offered support.

Thank you to Dr. Roberta Temes for her encouragement and for saying over and over in her writing class or by email to write and then rewrite and write again.

One big thank you: to Sister Judith's 8th grade class of 1965, St. Augustine, Newport, Rhode Island, for the friendship and all the memories we made at Rough Point.

And a final thank you to Doris Duke for letting a little girl's dream to come true.

INTRODUCTION

As a forward to my book, I'd like to share the background of my parents, Howard and Carman McFarlane. Both my parents were born in Canada and came from large families.

My dad was the oldest of ten children. As a young boy, he worked as a caddy and would often help take care of the golf course. At home, he would help his mom in her flower garden (I like to think it was their special time to be alone) and lend a hand to his dad in the large vegetable garden. Little did he know he was getting ready for his future career! He enjoyed the outdoor life of playing golf, hunting, and fishing. As most Canadians did, he learned to play hockey at a young age. During War World II he served in the Royal Canadian Air Force.

My mom was the second oldest child of a family of six

children, with her only brother being the eldest. Because my grandfather died when my mother was a very young child, each of the siblings was responsible for specific chores. Hers was to help with the cooking; her way of cooking was a pinch of this, a dash of that, and handful of this. That cooking style carried into adulthood.

They were married at a young age and had four children, three daughters and one son. My two sisters and I were born in Canada and my brother was born in New Jersey.

We moved to New Jersey during the summer of 1952. It must have been hard for them to leave family and friends behind but knowing that my mom had two sisters Irene and Stella who lived in New Jersey gave them some comfort.

Dad worked at many different types of jobs, at a golf course, as a groundskeeper and caddy and also at a steel mill company on the assembly line.

Mom used her cooking skills at a hotel, assisted in a nursing home, and cleaned private homes. Baking pies for people she met through family and friends members would bring in extra money.

EACH OF US HAS A STORY TO TELL

IT MAY BEGIN WITH

ONCE UPON A TIME

OR

A LONG TIME AGO

CHAPTER ONE

A LITTLE GIRL'S DREAM

My story begins as a little girl with a Big Dream. My dream was to live in a "Big House"; just like the one I would often see behind the towering trees on Route 22 in Martinsville, New Jersey where I lived during my child hood. As far back as I can remember, I would say to my parents, "Someday I am going to live in a house that big". Of course living in a trailer at that time, any house would seem big. But that house, that hidden-away house, always caught my eye. My dad would shake his head, smile, and say, "Someday." Little did I know that the Big House dream would come true! Instead of being hidden behind trees, the house would be surrounded by water and rocks. Cars would not be speeding as on Route 22 but instead they would be slowing down on the "Avenue" to get a glimpse of the house beyond the rock wall and the big, black iron gate.

To understand how a family from New Jersey moved to what they thought was the reopening of a small "summer cottage" in Newport, Rhode Island, we have to go back to a special job interview.

It was 1961 when my parents told me that they were going to a job interview that could possibly change our lives. I was informed that my younger brother, Benny, and I could go with them to the interview, but with a few conditions.

The interview was scheduled early on a Saturday morning, which unfortunately for me meant I could not sleep in or watch cartoons. Being ten years old, this didn't sit well with me.

The second condition meant my brother and I would have to stay in a guardhouse with someone we didn't know, the security guard. It felt as if I would be in captivity. "You are going to leave us with a stranger!" Was all I could think? My parents knew perfectly well that I was afraid of every little thing. Why would they even think of putting me in this situation? The only happy thought I had was that we would miss Catechism that weekend.

My mom was a great cook; baking pies was her specialty. She had a job cleaning our neighbor Anna's home on the days that Anna's friends came for their weekly bridge game. Mom usually brought a homemade pie and flowers from Dad's garden. Flowers decorated our house from spring until late fall. My dad had a green thumb with flowers and vegetables. He worked in the gardens after work and on weekends, taking such great pride in them. Anna often told her card-playing friend who worked at Duke's Farm about the couple whose wife cleaned her home, baked desserts, and her husband who loved to garden. From this friendship, the job interview emerged.

Driving to the interview I was bored by my parents' conversation:

Mom: "This will be a very special cottage"

Dad: "She is a very powerful woman".

Mom: "And rich, too."

My parents looked down at their cigarette packs and knew they were adding to her wealth as a tobacco heiress. I was born in Canada, so I knew the Queen of England was rich. I wondered about the owner of the summer cottage. Could she be as rich?

When we finally arrived, we pulled up to a rather large black iron gate. A man walked forward (quite grandly, I thought) dressed in a fine-looking uniform. Was this the man we were to stay with? He asked my parents their names and then said, "Children, come with me."

My brother and I got out of the car very slowly, looking at my parents as my mom gave us a smile that meant it was okay. Then, with a push of a button, the gates opened and my parents drove inside. I could see nothing beyond the rows of trees, only the tops of buildings. We went with the guard to wait for our parents' return. To our delight we entered the guardhouse and we saw a TV set. The guard told us we could watch what we wanted to, and that meant cartoons. He even had some treats for us, chocolate chip cookies and orange juice. While we waited in the guardhouse, the time seemed to fly by. Our parents ensured that one day we would get a glimpse of what was beyond the big, black gates of Duke Farms. That Saturday opened a new world for us!

My parents became caretakers of the Rough Point Estate, on Bellevue Avenue in Newport, Rhode Island the summer cottage of Doris Duke. I thought "No big deal. We'd be living in a summer cottage. And anyway, how big could this place possibly be?"

Dad would take care of the grounds and mom would take care of the interior during the winter and help with preparing and serving the meals in the summer. I thought this would be an easy job for Mom as she cleaned and cooked at other places and was always making pies for our family and friends. Dad enjoyed working in his garden. I thought again, how hard could this job really be?

CHAPTER TWO

GETTING READY FOR THE MOVE

Getting ready to move seemed so exciting in one way, meeting new friends, going to a new school and living in another state. Yet sad in another saying goodbye to friends was going to take a while, after all, being in fifth grade, you make a lot of friends along the way. In addition, I would really miss not seeing the neighbors who lived next to us. They had six girls and I could always find one of them to come out and play, go swimming, or have tea parties with our dolls under the many weeping willow trees in the summer. Not to mention the big tire tube swing that Dad had put up on one of the trees down by the patio. Then in the winter, we would either go ice skating or sled riding. Would I ever reconnect with the friends who lived on Vosseller Avenue or Tullo Road in Martinsville? Would I be leaving that certain someone behind and would we reconnect in years to come? There were so many thoughts I would be thinking and dreaming, and wondering. Would any of my little girl thoughts and dreams come true in years to come?

Then the hardest part came -- saying goodbye to my two sisters Nita and Audrey. Since they were nine and ten years older than me, they did not make the move with us. Saying good-bye to Stella, my only girl cousin (who is six months older than me) here in New Jersey was hard. To say the goodbyes to Chuck and Larry my two older boy cousins was a little easier (as they often played tricks on me or scared me to make me cry) and my younger cousin, Peter. Making me cry was not a very hard thing to do, as after we watched scary movies they would hide and jump out behind a chair and make noises. I had just finished studying the New England states in school, so I knew my new home would be a distance from Berkeley Heights and Springfield where my cousins lived.

My parents and other relatives reassured me that they would come for visits or that we would come back. We were only going to be a few hours away, but that did not ease my mind. I knew deep down that the visits would be few and far between. No more Saturday night sleepovers or a Sunday afternoon drive for family dinners. To me, it meant moving away and that was a very big deal.

The night before we moved, my sister Audrey gave Benny and I each a silver dollar. My dad put my brother's dollar on a key chain and a few years later a guest at Rough Point borrowed the car keys and lost them. The keys were replaced, but not the silver dollar. It is sad to say that no one thought to replace that unique gift. To the guest, it may have only been a silver dollar. To my brother, his dollar, his sister's gift to him, was lost.

My parents told us we would have an entire floor to live on and that household products and our food were provided by Miss Duke. Mom left many of her dishes with relatives or friends. She only brought the items that meant the most to her. Mom and Dad told us we could not bring all of our toys, only special ones, and just the ones that we really played with and loved. Since we drove a small car at the time, and we could not fit everything in it, a truck from Duke Farms that was headed to Newport came and took our items. I took my two favorite big dolls and some small items that were special to me. My bike was left behind. At the time, it did not seem fair and even now, I say it was not fair. I remember the spacious truck and I thought, both then and today that my bike could have been squeezed in between the antique paintings or vases. The bike was a hand me down from my cousin but I still wanted it. I do hope the six girls who lived next door to us got great use from our cast offs. Dad promised he would get me another bike in the spring or summer. And I held him to that promise.

CHAPTER THREE

THE MOVING DAY

The big moving day took place on February 15th, 1961. For a few nights before the move, we stayed at my Aunt Irene's house in Berkeley Heights, New Jersey. We were up early the day we moved -- laughing, crying and having breakfast with cousins before it was off to Springfield to Aunt Stella's house. We found a lunch all packed for us, said our final good-bye and set out on our new adventure.

I did not see the truck that came and got our items. As I said before, our family car at the time was a small car. Normally there was just enough room to look out the window. Now with the car filled with so many boxes, we had even less room. That proved to be a good thing now that I think about it. It gave my brother and me less room to argue about being on the other one's side.

Driving up Interstate 95 seemed to take forever. We had gone this way before traveling to Canada. Time seemed to go so much faster. Of course, dad traveled at night so he would not get the big famous question over and over again, "Are we there yet?" We stopped only for gas and to use the restroom. The long wait in lines to pay for tolls and bridges upset Dad, since he wanted to get to Newport before the truck arrived. We got lost a few times which added more stress to Dad's attitude. To help make the time go by quicker, I tried to picture the cottage. Would trees surround our new home? Would an arch of ivy be covering the front door?? Would we come upon a wooden gate and follow a rock path leading us up to the door?

Bringing me back to the real world, Dad asked me to keep track of each toll and bridge, so he would be reimbursed for the money he spent. I thought to myself I wish he had told me this before we started. Paper would have been better than writing the amounts on one of the boxes in crayon!

Seeing the sign for "Welcome to Rhode Island" meant we were finally here! At least, I hoped we were. We then saw a sign for the Jamestown Ferry. We needed to take a ferryboat ride! No one told me we were going on a ferry and I thought, "Great, how long is this going to take?" To make matters even worse, we had just missed the boat by a few minutes. Since this was winter, the wait would mean an hour for the next one to arrive. When all these things happened Dad got really upset, since all he was thinking of was the truck and wanting to be there for the unloading. He was probably also thinking it wouldn't look good starting a new job and arriving so late. What were we to do for a whole hour, just sit and wait? We did not want to get out of line and drive around to see any of the sights here. As with our luck, not knowing what to see or where to go, we would miss the next boat.

However, once on the ferry, it was not so bad. We went outside, got up on the deck, and watched as the boat pulled away. It sure was cold and you felt each of the waves as you went over them. As we pulled into the dock, everyone felt the ferry hit up against the pilings and we were surprised when the spray of water hit our faces. We noted the ferry schedule and how many cars it could hold so relatives and friends could be told what to expect when they came to visit.

By the time we got to Newport, it was early evening and darkness had fallen so we did not see much of the city. All we knew about Rough Point was that it was the last house on the left side of Bellevue Avenue. We drove up the short winding servant's driveway with high hedges on the sides. My heart pounded and my head wondered what would be waiting for us.

We were welcomed by a gentleman with a big brown dog by his side. They were waiting for us on the partially open wooden back porch. He introduced himself to us and told us his name was Mr. G, a painter who came up from Duke Farms and the dog was named Shep. Stone walls (the same ones as on the Avenue) forming an arch on either side of the porch. It was sad to say no trees bending over to form an arch. No little rock path existed that would lead up to the house. The driveway was gravel, so I decided that could be my rock path. I must admit I was a little disappointed. I had a picture of a cottage in my mind and it looked like one in a storybook with a fairy tale ending. I guess I read too many of those books. My dad seemed to be quite happy because we got there before the truck. I guess it was good we had those few boxes of clothes with us so we could change. Late that night, the truck came with the rest of our belongings. After a little snack Mr. G asked us:

"Would you like to get a tour of the main part of the house?" A big "Yes" was the answer.

CHAPTER FOUR

BEYOND THE KITCHEN

The first room was the butler's pantry; it was a rather large room, with a very long and wide brown polished table. Looking straight ahead of us was two very tall windows and below a sink between two counters. A dishwasher was to the right of the sink. I do not remember the dishwasher ever being used. On opposite sides of the table were old fashioned brown iceboxes, warming ovens, and cupboards filled with beautiful china. Mr. G was pointing to the pull-up wooden window where the maids could easily pass items through or talk to each other instead of going around to the kitchen. One cabinet was always filled with blue cans of macadamia nuts. To this day, I never recalled anyone eating them but they were always being bought.

Seeing a doorway in front of us, I wondered where it

was going to lead us. When the door finally opened, I discovered it was a safe! Wait! Wow! Is this where we will see all the gold or jewelry? But only the polished silver was there. A walk-in closet with shelves was to the left of us where, at times, wine would often be kept. Also on the wall to the left was a phone that we learned was a private line to some of the rooms. When the buzzer sounded, it was a signal that Miss Duke or one of her guests needed a maid or maid's attention. The phone was to be answered quickly -- very quickly! I wondered how quickly they would react. Will it be like children racing, first one to answer is the winner? Who is this woman? Who has this power that when a phone rings people will act so quickly? I thought to myself, a very wealthy person must live here and what kind of person? What was she like? I guess I will just have to wait and see. Little did I know what would welcome us?

CHAPTER FIVE

BEYOND THE BIG BROWN DOORS OF

THE BUTLERS'S PANTRY

The doors began to open! I thought we would see beautiful furniture, with bright colored walls and thick, softly colored carpet. With all these different thoughts rushing through my head and my heart racing, the door opened to a dark, cold room covered in sheets. Yes, every inch of the room was covered in white. It was like looking at different sizes of ghosts. We did learn that sheets were on the furniture to keep the dust off them. Even the walls had rugs on them! What was this all about? What was this room called? Were all the rooms so dark and cold? I got a feeling that I was not welcome and I should turn around and go back to New Jersey. We learned it was the dining room. I thought to myself, does someone really want to eat in here? The only warm feeling you would get would be from the fireplace. Just one room after another and all were dark and covered in sheets. Even the hallways had sheets on everything.

Then we came to a room filled with all windows called the solarium. Finally, we entered a room that felt peaceful and welcoming. This was a room my dad came to love and enjoy. In here, he grew tall geraniums. They were the tallest geraniums that I ever saw; to this day I have never seen anyone else grow them that tall. The only problem was this loud strange noise. No one else seemed to be concerned and then I heard it again. It seemed so far away but yet, so close. Again, I heard something and again no one was concerned. Maybe I was the only one who heard it. Maybe I was hearing things, but then I thought that someone else must have heard it also. Would I ever find out what or where the noise is? I found out years later, this was a room a few of my friends came to enjoy.

The ballroom was next. This was a room where I could picture the ladies wearing long gowns of many colors, with matching shawls or capes and long white gloves. They curtsied as they took their partner's hand as if in a fairy tale ball. Oh, I could not wait to see if any of this would happen! Mr. G was busy working in here, telling my parents all about the wallpaper. I thought this wasn't a big deal (he was a painter so he was very interested in how each piece of the paper paneling was put on). It's just green with birds and more sheets. Little did I realize that years from now, in this very room, we would have our last family Christmas picture taken?

When was this tour going to end? I was bored with room after room covered in sheets, even the hallway. How many more rooms could there be and would they all be covered in white? One of the rooms on the right was the women's powder room and a short distance to the left and going down a few steps was the men's room.

As we came to the short hallway you could see the front entrance. On either side of the door were tall armored shining knights. Wow, this place is more like a castle, not a cottage! When coming back to the hallway, I noticed the marble floors and thought; "Hey this would be neat to slide on!" Not that that would ever really happen. Would it?

Even the grand staircase was covered in sheets. Being so

big, it seemed more like a room instead of a hallway. The windows were so high and wide, some even tinted. I thought, "What a nice banister to slide down." I wondered how many seconds it would take someone to slide down from the top to the bottom. (Good thing nobody read my mind). Going up the stairway, rather large pictures, or, as they like to say, portraits were hung. Each was placed just so; little detail was pointed out. One was of a little girl with blonde hair dressed in white with a blue ribbon around her waist. Her eyes looked so sad, and, in a strange way' they seemed to be watching every move I made. We learned it was Miss Duke when she was twelve years old. Years later, I learned how she would have to pose for days to have the portrait done and she wanted so much to play with her friends at the beach. Wow! She was a child just like me who wanted to have fun. It would also be the last portrait she would have done before her dad died. She did admit, when she was much older, that it was her favorite one and was happy to have it done for him. On either side of her were portraits of her parents, James and Nanaline Inman Duke

At the top of the stairs we came to a room decorated all

in purple. Everywhere you looked, you saw purple except the bed. It was RED. A big red headboard and I wondered what my old art teacher would have thought of that interesting combination. We did find a rug and it was so thick and soft and yes, purple. The room was so different from all the other rooms. It was so bright and so pretty. This room belonged to Miss Duke. At one time, it was her mother's. The room was so big. A mother- of- pearl secretary desk was to the left of the bed. So many other items here in the room were made of mother- of- pearl. They were all so different, and pretty in their own way. Wait! What did I see? Yes, two phones and one was the private line. How many more can I find on this floor? Had I missed any down- stairs? On either side of the walls were two big walk-in closets with built- in- pull -out drawers with a few clothes in them. But the ones there were so soft and bright; especially the bathing suit cover- up in a lime green. Over in the corner, all stacked up, were many different kinds of magazines.

The bathroom was next, and what a different room! Big black and white square tiles and gold- color faucets decorated the room. But something was missing- the toilet. Everyone has a toilet. A door was open. There, in the room, it was all by itself. We were told that Miss Duke wanted her privacy. Had a maid really walked in unexpected? Truth or rumor, I never knew for sure.

Leaving here, we went into Mr. Duke's room. Wow, wait a minute, a Mr. and a Mrs. Room. Now that seemed a little different, but maybe only to me. To me, this room gave the appearance of always being so dark, creepy, and cold. A room you would not want to enter by yourself, or stay for any length of time. Even the bed was creepy looking, so big and the tall bed post made it look so old fashioned. A style of bed you would find in movies of old castles and yet Mr. Duke's room was the only room on the floor with a TV. I remember a very cool scale was built in the bathroom floor, which was the only neat thing to remember.

Leaving the room by another entrance I saw a short hallway and a closed door to the left. The door was really a big double doorway painted in white. All I thought of was a really special room must be here and be so beautiful to have such a big door. No, there I go getting ahead of myself. We were then told it leads to the living quarters of the servants.

Oh, the tour is over, I thought but instead we went to the right and found ourselves in front of Miss Duke's room. A set of lights over the bedroom door were pointed out to us. Mr. G informed us lights on meant Entertaining. Do not come in. Did someone come in without permission? Big deal. There wasn't even a TV in the room, I thought. How could you be entertained? I never knew what the lights meant until many years later.

Leaving the room, we came to one small room on the left and we discovered it was the music room. The room was very dark with a piano, a small sofa, and a couple of chairs. The drapes were dark gold, which made the room even darker. Hidden in the dark paneled walls were closets, which made me think a safe could be hidden there. However, it was just closets.

Miss Duke often practiced both singing and playing the piano here; this was the only room on the left side of the long narrow hallway with a very low ceiling. The wallpaper was in blue with water in the background and Incas dressed in their native attire. It reminded me of a page from a social studies book. Across the hallway was a small bedroom with a few stairs.

Floor length drapes framed either side of the stairs that would lead to the bathroom.

The next groups of rooms were set off by a short stairway and each was different in style. The first room on the left was so dark in color and had hardly any furniture. Next was a very large room painted in a light color and the trim painted in different colors of pastels. It was my mom's favorite bedroom. Another room was small in size but with beautiful furniture. It had a mother- of- pearl bed with bright flower wallpaper- a room any little girl would love. Mr. G spoke a little bit about the rooms and named a few guests who slept in them.

Coming back and going to the end of the hallway, a door opened and there it was- the most magnificent room I ever saw. It had soft red wallpaper and a large dark canopy bed. This was a room fit for a queen or king, I thought. All I kept thinking was" Oh the guest who sleeps in this room must be so special." I couldn't wait to see who it would be. As it turned out the room belonged to Miss Duke as a child. Something seemed strange. There were no closets and, yes, a story was told. The story goes, she woke early and dressed herself and her governess did not approve of the wardrobe. So the closets were taken out and put in the hallway outside her room.

We were then taken to the fourth floor where we spent our first night. By going this way from the main part of the house, we completely missed the third floor (where we were to live for the next three years). The fourth floor had rows of bedrooms and one large bathroom with one really large room where years later Mr. Tirella (a close friend of Miss Duke) would work and store many of his paintings. In a year or so, the room would be used to store Miss Duke's nephew's toys. We were given strict orders not to play with any of them. It did not seem fair to see all these toys not played with and so many were games, but we really did listen and did not touch them. I do remember going to the room a few times to find out what kind of toys he had. All I remember now were toy soldiers and a couple of board games. Many of the rooms had one or two single beds, a dresser or two, and a few wicker rocking chairs. Every room was very plain with no fancy decorations. It reminded me a lot of a hospital ward in a movie with Shirley Temple where she had gone looking for her father during wartime.

CHAPTER SIX

WOW!!!!!!!! DO WE REALLY LIVE HERE!!

The next day I thought, "Wow, what a view to wake up to!" Hardly any trees were here; only water, rocks, and more water. I went running down the hallway to the next floor, then another floor with a short hallway and then came to the first floor and off to find the kitchen. Upon entering the kitchen, we were introduced to another man named Mr. J. He lived off the estate and he would be working with Dad. He had worked at Rough Point for a few years, and would continue working at the estate for another few years. Coming back and forth to work, he drove what looked like a wooden station wagon that belonged to the estate; the back was completely cut off. I never saw a car like that before. When I first saw it, I thought it belonged to him and he assured me it did not. Was he embarrassed to drive the car?

Was that the reason he tried to assure me it wasn't his? At times, when Dad used the car he would drop me off at school and then he would proceed to take items to the dump I was so embarrassed. Because I recall saying, "Oh you can drop me off a few blocks from school to save yourself some time and get to the dump early". I really don't think he bought that story because right in front of school he would drop me off. In the next couple of years, new trucks would be bought and those living off the estate would use their own cars for going back and forth to work.

  Seeing the kitchen in daylight it looked so different from the night before. I noticed a second sink on a shorter wall, slightly hidden behind the stove. The stove was so long that it covered one wall. Boxes of long stick matches and white crackers that were shaped like a circle filled the top shelf. The burners had handles to be lifted up. Do we add wood or coal to light it? When I think of that stove now, old-fashioned pops in my mind and I remember the crackers stored on top. As I recall, we never ran out of the crackers. I do not remember ever eating them. Could that have been the reason the shelf was always well-stocked? A small table was in front of one the windows. This is where Benny and I would sit and look out the window at the ocean view. This gave us a place where we could eat and talk and be by ourselves, especially in the summer when the summer help came. There was a very long wooden table in the middle of the room and off in the corner was a big wicker rocking chair. Top and bottom cabinets were on one wall. Another small table was set against a small wall. The freshly squeezed orange juice would be made here. That is really something, a table only for orange juice. That just seemed like a big waste, but then again it was not my place to say anything and I was not the one squeezing all the oranges. On the other hand, I was not getting any of it to drink. The kitchen floor had small black and white tiles. (These would be used as a model of a snowflake for a science project later that spring) A small room was off the kitchen and it was called the maid's pantry. It was a long narrow room with many cabinets and built-in drawers and on one side was a small wooden pull- up window door that was connected to the butler's pantry. It was the same window door Mr. G had shown us the night before, but somehow it looked so much different from the other side.

The help's dining room was located just before the kitchen. I got a warm feeling as you stepped into the room. In fact, it could have been because of the fireplace that I saw as I entered. In the room was a big square dark brown table. On one side of the blue painted wall were sliding cabinet doors and built- in drawers. In addition, another sink was hidden behind a colorful blue canvas wall screen. The screen was kept there all year long. Of course, not to forget, there were more wicker rocking chairs and the big dark color green leather sofa.

On the opposite side of the hallway across from the help's dining room and kitchen two other little rooms were also on this floor plus a small closet. One room was called the flower room. I thought a flower room was a room just for flowers. What we found in here was a small closet, a small sink, a worktable and one wall filled with shelves that went straight up to the ceiling. On the top shelf were small empty wine bottles. Empty? Yes. Why, who knows? I never knew or cared to find out why, but they sure came in handy years later for holding candles at slumber parties. One future classmate kept a bottle going into her adulthood. During the summer however, this room would be used quite often.

The other was called the vegetable room. All I found in here was another table, a sink and an old-fashioned icebox. Why was it called a vegetable room? It never had any vegetables stored in there. Was it a room only to wash them? I guess years ago names were given to rooms for washing vegetables and cutting flowers. Who really knows the reason the rooms have such names, one for only flowers and one for vegetables. Seemed like all the rooms had one thing in common and that would be a sink. I guess I never had to worry about where to wash my hands. The only room missing on this floor was a bathroom.

Next, it was off to explore the basement. The hallway was not very long and only a door was on one side. Wow a whole wall, even though it was not very long and it was only a door. You know I had to ask where this would lead us. With a very firm voice, we were told it was an old dumb waiter elevator, and that the door was to be kept locked at all times. This type of elevator used ropes only. In a few years to come, it would come in handy. Oh, wait and what do we find here, before going down the stairs but another outside side door. Do I dare say now "Wow "to myself since this door came in handy years later for someone who was a little sick and coming in a little late. On the other hand, it might have been useful for workers showing up late for work and saying, "I was here," or those who slipped out the side door or slipped in the side door. However, you look at it; the door was handy at times.

Once in the basement, we found that it was divided into many parts. The first section had many little rooms and two big rooms. In one of the big rooms, we found the washing machine, a long table and some long metal handles in a wall. What are the handles, you ask? Mr. G took the handles and gave them a firm tug. As the doors were opened, we wondered what it would be. All you saw were long metal racks. It was explained that the metal rods on the racks are where you would place your clothes to dry. A dryer that goes in the wall. Now that is something different! A place like this and no clothes dryer that spins items dry. The other big room had tables and ironing boards, and in the middle was a black spin machine. This would come in handy later when I was in high school to wring my sweaters out. A few bathrooms were also here. The other part of the cellar was so dark. It didn't have windows like the other side and it had so many little rooms that could be used for a nice game of hide and seek, except for one little thing. (To me it was a big thing) The basement then had quite a lot of mice running around. At the very end of the basement was a big room, a great big room. A room for a swimming pool, I was thinking (which did not come until after I moved out). This room was where my dad let my brother and I shoot our bow and arrows. Living out in the country in New Jersey, we were used to shooting them, but that was outside. Here we had a room with a target on the wall.

Off we went to run around outside. What a view! The water and the rocks were so close, but the amazing thing was when you turned around and saw the house that this was not a "summer cottage" but a "castle," a really big castle. We had so much to take in. Once outside, I could take in the whole view of the house. I saw the white statues of lions on the steps in front of the solarium. In addition, looking around I saw some parts of the house had ivy growing on it. So in a way it was a "cottage," but not the kind I had imagined. We ran and rolled down the hills, feeling the breeze and mist from the water. But wait, what was that smell coming from the water and what was all that green or black stuff all over the rocks? When going down to the rocks to jump on them, I could see the seaweed. So that was the smell. The noise we heard the night before in the solarium was the waves hitting against the rocks. The waves were so high that many times the whitecaps could be seen from the house. Being on the cliffs, I could see many other big houses, or are they also called" summer cottages"? Some parts of the cliffs had a drop of seventy feet to the water. I would never be able to touch the water. I wonder if this is the reason I am now afraid of heights. A little wooden bridge was on one part of the cliff. It had a stone wall on either side as I went to step on the bridge. Did this cliff have a name? I think now I am going to like this place. When would we meet our neighbors and would they have children to play with? Would their houses have all their rooms covered in sheets? Dad was outside and I was sure was getting ideas of how the gardens would look. Mom was busy in the house and I was sure thinking, "What have we gotten ourselves into?"

After a full day of exploring the grounds, we were off to the third floor to settle in. This floor was to be our home for the next three years. I had a small room painted in white with three small windows that overlooked the driveway. One part of the ceiling slanted. It was the perfect spot for my first vanity table that had a long beige skirt, with pink trim and a glass top. It fit perfectly between my two white metal frame single beds. My parent's room was rather large, and also painted in white. Their room had a beautiful view overlooking the front lawn and the ocean. My brother's room overlooked the ocean and rocks. To reach his room you walked down a long narrow hallway. One of the walls had a built- in shelves where he could put all his toys and books. It was just perfect for a boy in second grade. The hallway was big enough to be used as a bedroom or sitting room. It was right next to the elevator. One extra room on the third would be used for storage; it had a hidden ladder in the room. Our bathroom was rather large with a really big walk- in closet where we had shelves. In fact, our bathroom was the only bathroom that had a shower.

CHAPTER SEVEN

MEETING THE LADY OF THE HOUSE

One Sunday in early spring, my parents got a call from Duke Farms that the Lady, as they called her, was to arrive that afternoon along with a guest. Therefore, in a very polite way, Benny and I were asked to stay at friend's houses for the afternoon. I am sure they must have arranged with the parents to keep us for so long. Therefore, off we went, each to a different house to play. I can remember thinking, "What am I going to miss? Will she arrive in the biggest white limo or the biggest black Rolls Royce I ever saw? And would she be wearing a long dress, a pillbox hat with a feather in it, and be wrapped in a fur coat with gold chains peeking out of the coat? Or possibly wearing a scarf with a gold brooch and holding onto a long cigarette holder? Would her guest be in a black pin- stripe tuxedo and be wearing black shiny shoes? The chauffer, would he be dressed in a light grey suit with a cap on his head, and quickly opens her door and extends his hand to help her out? As you can tell, I watch too many old movies. What fun I had dreaming all this up in my head. Did I really miss all of this? After our day of play, the questions would be answered and oh, what a shock I would get with those answers. No limo or long dress or tuxedo my parents informed me. "Mom, are you sure you are telling me the truth about what she wore? A pair of blue jeans and a tee shirt!" I couldn't believe it. My parents informed me that an old car came pulling up in the driveway and when the male driver got out, my dad informed them they must leave as the Lady of the house would be arriving shortly. The female passenger quickly got out of the car, her hand stretched out to them, said, "Hi, Mr. and Mrs. McFarlane. I am Doris Duke and this is my friend."

CHAPTER EIGHT

SPRING

When spring arrived, we met new friends and had them come over and play. Family and friends came down from Canada or up from New Jersey. One Sunday, I ran in the house with some chocolate eggs and my dad asked where I got them. I told him a family was hiding eggs. They said they had done this for the last few years and they let me help the children find them. He seemed to get upset that strangers would come up on the property. I explained that they came on only a small portion of the property. Phone calls were made back and forth to the farm about a fence being put up, but for now more signs were posted: "Private Property -Do Not Trespass ". A fence meant not being able to go down on the rocks to play or throw pebbles in the water. Years later a fence would be installed.

On many early evenings, Benny and I went fishing with my dad on the rocks. Fishing was not my favorite thing to do. However, it was fun to go out on the rocks and climb around on them. Especially on the ones where we could only go with an adult being present. Nevertheless, I must say it was different and kind of fun to put the crabs on the line instead of worms. A few years later my sister, Audrey came to visit. Dad would get her to go fishing with him. They would go out on the docks. I wondered why. Was it because with age you realize how dangerous the rocks could be? That was just fine with me as I had the chance to play with my nieces Lynn and Dawne.

Newport was a large Navy town back in the sixty's and seventy's. Living so close to the water, I was able to see the ships as they were returning to dock. We became familiar with the ships and knew which classmates would be absent from school the next day as it meant their dad would be back from sea duty.

Rules were set down with the spring ending: no playing on the front lawn; and no friends were to come over during the week. Would we be able to play on the back lawn or were we to stay upstairs and out of sight? What would two children do without making some kind of noise? What was this with all these rules? Wasn't this our home? We were informed by our parents that, yes, this was our home where we lived but not our house. Okay, so it was Miss Duke's house but what were we going to do for the summer? We were given strict orders not to go swimming off the rocks by ourselves. We thought that was just great. We had all this water and no swimming.

Mom was busy in the house taking off all the white sheets covering the furniture and neatly storing them away, dusting and putting fresh linens on all the beds. By now, she knew the names of the guests and a little bit about them. Each room seemed to have its own personality. This job would take almost the whole spring.

The main part of the house looked so different with all the sheets off. The dining room was so big and had hardly any furniture. As I entered the room, I came upon a large dark bendable screen with a table in front of it where the maids would often set up the next course that would be served. One time when my sisters were up from New Jersey, they hid behind it to try to get a glimpse of Miss Duke. Over in front of the windows was a very long table with only a few chairs. Now the room had a warm feeling and the fireplace was not even on. Next came the morning room, it had a small sofa and a very low coffee table, where the newspapers were often placed. There was also, a table in front of the window and all it ever had on it was the telephone, pad of paper, pen and the extra phone line. Over in the corner was a ship inside a fish tank or it looked like a tank to me? The tank was as big as a coffee table. Why is this name given to this room? Was it only used in the morning? As I recall, it was used quite often in the evening after dinner. Again, rooms have names and it must have had a reason at one time. The great hallway had a rug in the middle of the room that we were given strict orders not to step on. It was called the 50-cent rug. Why? Did anyone really pay that amount when they stepped on it? The yellow room was next and yellow it was- a very soft yellow with some white trim. Hanging down in the middle of the room was the biggest chandelier I ever saw. This room was so much brighter than any of the other rooms. Was this a room or just a hallway?

Was it here the whole time? How could I have missed such a welcoming room, so calm and peaceful? When it was covered in sheets, the warmth and glow of the room had been taken away. Miss Duke would use the room as a passing hallway either going into the ballroom or solarium. Is it from the color of this room that yellow was to become one of my favorite colors? The room to me was so calming and to be used only for passing through was such a waste of a beautiful room. It was years before we did learn that Mrs. Duke would use the room quite often for her sitting room where she would sit at her desk by the window and write out many of her invitations to her dinner parties. A small sofa and chairs were on either side of the fireplace. The ballroom was the room I find the most interesting. The grand piano, a harp, such tall vases, many small groups of little chairs and each one had a story on the back and on the seat. On one end was a big golden clock and on both sides of the walls were long wide mirrors with a few big chandeliers. It was such an extraordinary room that could hold so many people and yet was hardly ever used. This room was always being decorated with items coming and going to Miss Duke's other homes and then coming back sometime later. One jazz musician who often visited would use the grand piano that was to the left of the room. The harp would have the sweetest sounds coming from it whenever it was used. A few times, I could hear the music.

Each of the bedrooms on the second floor had a different design with one thing in common. In each vanity drawer was writing paper in light blue with Rough Point printed in dark blue at the top.

Dad was outside busy with the gardens. Busy with trimming hedges, roto tilling, digging and mapping out where the bulbs and seeds were going to go. Seed packets and bulbs were coming in by mail all the time. Each morning and late afternoon, he would rake the sidewalk outside the main gate since gravel would get on it. This would be done from the early spring until early fall. His day would begin very early before it got too hot. In the early evening, he would be back working in the gardens by himself again.

CHAPTER NINE

THE FIRST SUMMER

By the beginning of summer, the help was arriving from New Jersey and New York. For a few summers, the maids stayed on the second floor. On this floor were six bedrooms, a walk-in linen closet, and one bathroom. A private bathroom was in one of the rooms, which was separated a distance from the other rooms. We were told it was a certain cook's room. Even though we would not meet until years later, it was always called her room.

The fourth floor was hardly ever used by the help. When male workers came from Duke Farms, they would stay on that floor. Lunch would be served roughly around noon in the help's dining room for all and it would be the big meal of the day. Around 4:30 in the afternoon, a light dinner would be served.

When the help was all settled in, you could sit and listen to the memories they had of Mrs. Duke when she would come. They would say how different in taste mother and daughter were. All I can remember thinking was who this person who owns this house was and is it really going to be different living here? How were we to act around her? Would we meet famous people, such as movie stars or royalty? Within a few days I would meet her and some of her guests.

She was a very tall, slender woman with long, thin, straight blonde hair who spoke with a soft voice. Often one of the maids would arrive with her. And she was called her personal maid. You did not see much of the maid, as she usually stayed in the main part of the house with Miss Duke. At times, she would appear and often say the time has been changed for dinner. With that, she would turn and go to pick out clothes or brush Miss Duke's hair. I kept thinking; "Wow, a maid just for brushing hair!"

The very first time that Dad picked Miss Duke up at the airport, she came with so many suitcases. I saw cashmere sweater sets in every color I could imagine. The clothes would stay at Rough Point. Mom was told she had one each of the same type of sweater sets in all her other homes. In the day time I often saw her wearing a bathing suit or the lime green beach cover up, a pair of sneakers, sunglasses, and a straw hat or a pair of jeans and a brightly colored tee shirt. Thinking back now, I do recall seeing her in a pair of shorts, although she usually wore a bathing suit. In the evening I would see her in a nice pair of slacks, with one of the cashmere sweater sets and often a gold cuff bracelet and a few times, a necklace. I never saw her wear anything glamorous. One time, I remember two pairs of wool slacks shrank and she gave them to me. They were so soft and kept me warm. I was only 4 feet 11 inches and she was over 6 feet tall. Those slacks really had to shrink a lot! Not sure if the cleaners who did the damage ever had her business again, but I thank them very much because the slacks did get a lot of use from me and I would tell many people who it was that gave them to me.

A rented car would be waiting for her here at the house and Miss Duke or one of her guests would drive the car. She never rented any fancy car. A few times a car would be driven up from the farm. Miss Duke and her guests enjoyed going to the Newport Folk and Jazz Festivals. Either on the day or day after Miss Duke arrived. A truck would also arrive from the farm with many crates of antique items. With the arrival, you would find Miss Duke busy rearranging items and deciding which ones would be sent back to the farm. To me, some of the items looked the same because in another few weeks they would be back up and be placed in a different room. One of her favorites was of a sleeping baby that was on the side table in the great hall. The maids said they were told to touch the little guy whenever they would walk by it. Did they really touch the little guy or is this another one of the tales that were told? I never found why or if they really did.

The kitchen was the perfect room to be in when gazing out at the water. I was able to see the many sailboats go by. The water could look so peaceful at times and then, with a blink of an eye, it would be roaring with the spray from the whitecaps coming up over the lawn. The smell of seaweed was not easily forgotten, even after moving away all these years later.

All the gardens were so pretty. On the front lawn that year, and only that year, was a round display garden with miniature flowers. Shades of pink and purple petunias were intertwined around white ones with pansies in the middle. Outlining the pastels were sweet alyssums going from whites to pinks and purples. The main gardens were hidden behind the neatly trimmed tall, rounded arch hedges with the sunflowers peeking overhead. As I entered the garden, the roses greeted me, forming their own arch. Since they were over seven feet in height anyone could easily walk under and meet their loved one waiting for them at the end of the aisle. At one end of the garden to the left, surrounded by its own little cove of a hedge, was a white statue. On either side of the arch, were flowers in more colors than one could imagine. One side, for example, would be filled with miniature snapdragons ranging from pink pastels to brightly colored pinks, and then going up in height to deep shades of purples with the bold colors of the gladiolas and dahlias in the back. The other side would be, as I like to think of it, the Wild Flower Garden. With the cornflowers, black- eyed Susan's, chrysanthemums, asters, or zinnias, and not to forget, my favorite -the daisies, each bending and swaying to me as if they were saying, "Pick me, play with me". What fun I had thinking of picking the petals off the daisies and saying, he loves he loves me not, and then to throw the middle up in the air. On second thought, better not. Surrounded on both sides were the vibrant orange colors of the marigolds or the small gerbera daisies. The rows of flowers were planted, so that when one was picked the next one would soon bloom. Queen Anne's lace and yarrow were found at the far back to the right of the garden that reminded me of weeds and, sad to say, it still does. Ferns and hosta were planted in the form of a diamond in the middle of the garden. Flowers were often picked and arranged by Miss Duke and would be seen throughout the house.

    The vegetable garden was on the side of the house just beyond the back driveway. Dad would often give me fifty cents to help him weed the garden. That may not sound like a lot of money, but after all fifty cents was fifty cents. Any table scraps were put on the compost pile and would be used in the soil of the garden that fall. One year, my dad grew pumpkins. That was the fall my nieces came up. Not sure if this is true or not, but I heard that this was the first time that Miss Duke ate beet greens. Beet greens are the top of the beets; some say it tastes sweeter then spinach. I know it was not my favorite vegetable to eat at that time and it still is not. Mint was also grown in the garden and would be used in the ice tea, which was freshly brewed every day.

For dinner, Miss Duke and her guests would start with a fresh salad, some kind of fish or chicken and assortment of vegetables would follow. I never saw any red meat being prepared. Dessert would be a freshly baked piece of pie with a wedge of cheese or fresh fruit. While I was living there, no big parties were ever held. It would be Miss Duke and a few guests. A few times, Mom did cook dinner and one of Miss Duke's favorites was a chicken dish made with mayonnaise and cheese. With all of the different meals served, certain china would be used. My favorite china was the white with the gold trim. Mom worked hard along with the other maids, staying up so late to serve dinner and then having to clean up. Then she was up early the next day to start all over again. Looking back, no wonder on some Fridays when Miss Duke would often leave to go to the farm they would just sit back and relax in the kitchen. They didn't relax too long since Monday would soon be here. They wore white uniforms and white shoes. No aprons or little white lacy caps were worn like on one of the TV shows where the server bowed to her employers as she slowly backed up and walked away. I guess I did watch TV way too much but then, it's kind of fun to think about it that way.

Accounts were set up at different stores. One of the accounts I really remember was at a hardware store. They gave Dad some nice thank you gifts (one especially was a small television set for my brother and me the Christmas of 1967. I even had that TV when I got married). One of the grocery stores would get a check each month or when the account got below a certain amount (that happened even when Miss Duke was not there). Fresh fruit would often be delivered a few times a week. Lobsters and other fresh fish would also be delivered. Only once did my dad make the mistake of eating the lobster that was left over from the night before. I guess even the rich like to eat certain special leftovers. Almost every day my brother and I would go uptown to get the newspaper with my dad. It was a small corner store off Broadway. When the buzzer in the butler's pantry would ring from the morning room, a maid knew it was time to bring the tray with the freshly squeezed orange juice and newspapers.

Still, surrounded with all this water, we could not go swimming. Mrs. N., one of the maids who worked their years ago under Mrs. Duke, informed us we were allowed to use Bailey's Beach. This was only a short distance from the house. A beautiful beach it was as the waves were so calm and the sand so soft. It was such a big difference from swimming in the brook like I did with the kids in New Jersey. I did not know that the beach had two separate sides until I once went over the invisible line and was informed to go back to my side as that side was for the well- to- do patrons of the beach. So I guess that is why the cabanas were over on that side. I never made that mistake again. How could Mrs. N forget to tell me to stay on the side with the high wall?

Late that summer we would understand the dangers of swimming off the rocks. One day after coming home from a day at the beach, we were happily greeted with a hug and kiss from my parents and the maids. We were to call the maids Mrs. or Miss, never by their first name. I think I knew only the last names of two of the maids. This was strange, a hug by everyone, even Mrs. E (and she was not that friendly) and Mrs. N just held my hand and cried. But one maid was missing. Where was Miss C? She always waited for us when we came home, waiting to hear how our day went. My mom took us aside and told us Miss C. had been sunbathing on the rocks and a wave came over her and she drowned. Nothing else was ever said of her after that day. We really did listen, because we never went on the rocks alone to go swimming again. Most of the maids stayed for the entire summer, but a few would go back and forth to Duke Farms to visit with family or work at the farm.

CHAPTER TEN

BACK TO HAVING FUN WITH FRIENDS

By fall, we were back into the old ways. My best friend Christine came over a lot to play. Christine lived on Lake View Avenue. It's a funny thing; Miss Duke owned a little house and a greenhouse on the same street. Once we were asked if our family would like to move to the little house. Would our life have been different if we had moved? At times, I would go over with my dad to check on the property. Once I remember being over there with my friend Christine playing and saw water going into the greenhouse. You would think I would have told my dad when I got home. Was the reason I did not say anything until the next day because I forgot or was it because I not supposed to be playing over in the yard? I never knew what ever happened to that property. That fall, I did get a brand new bike. On some

Saturdays, my brother and I would ride our bikes uptown to return the soda bottles and we got to keep the cash. How great was that!

I would find dad and his helper outside digging up the bulbs and putting on the shutters before the cold winter would set in. Mom would be in the main part of the house putting the white sheets on all the furniture.

Dad also had another job to do and that was to check every so often at a one of Miss Dukes friend's house. A few times, she gave Dad items for me. One was a music box; my one favorite gift was a little Swiss house that had a boy and girl coming out of the door. A few times, I went with Dad. Her house was a lot different from Miss Duke's. For instance, it was smaller and you got a welcome feeling when you entered.

That November, our family made the trip to New Jersey. I stayed with my cousins and my parents took my brother on to St. Joseph's Hospital in Philadelphia, Pennsylvania. When my parents went for the job interview the previous year, they informed Miss Duke that my brother needed to see doctors in Philadelphia. The trips were made in the fall and in the spring (the times Miss Duke wouldn't be there). Later I would learn Miss Duke made phone calls to Duke University doctors to see if they knew of any new treatments that could help him. (He had too many veins growing in one arm and this was causing harm to his heart). When he became an adult, he outgrew the condition, something my parents had always prayed for.

During the winter months we had our own hills for sleigh riding. It would be a few close friends, and it was great not to have to wait in lines for our turns. It seemed that we had our own private hills.

By the end of sixth grade, Christine would be moving; her dad was in the navy and would be transferred. We kept in touch by letters for a few years. I saw Christine twice after she moved as she had family who lived in Rhode Island and Massachusetts

CHAPTER ELEVEN

WOULD EACH YEAR BE THE SAME?

With each spring, Dad would get the gardens ready and would beam with pride with his new creations. More and more flowers were introduced. Mom would be busy in the main part of the house. Each year it seemed they had more work to do before the summer help came. With each summer, different help often came, along with the guests.

One summer I even babysat for one of the guest's two granddaughters. They would come up to my room and we would play dolls or board games. At the end of the evening, I would walk them back to the main part of the house and off they went to their rooms.

Seems with living here all this time, I got too used to waking up, going down for breakfast, going back upstairs and finding something to do. Was the house getting too boring or was I missing seeing my parents the way I did in the wintertime? They seemed to be out of sight and unavailable now.

With Christine moving away and going into seventh grade, I went to a new school and that meant meeting new friends. One new friend I knew from the beach. Claire is still a close friend and helped me with this book. Over the next few years, many of the girls came over for slumber parties. At the end of eighth grade, Mom and Dad let the class have a party on the lawn by the solarium. Many of them lived in the part of town that was called the Fifth Ward. This was not around the corner for me. It would be close to a forty-five minute walk each way. I even went to a new beach. Gooseberry Beach was a half hour walk, so much different than going down the block to Bailey's Beach. Gooseberry Beach had sand dunes, dressing rooms and a snack bar.

At times when my dad went down to Duke Farms, my brother Benny or I would go and we would spend the time at my cousin's house. A couple of times, a cousin would come back with us to Newport.

CHAPTER TWELVE

A MEMORY TO END THE SUMMER

The late summer of 1964, a prince from India came to Rough Point. I wanted to meet him so badly and kept asking when, when, when? I kind of knew what I was going to wear either my dress with the brightly colored flowers and the pink bow in the back, or my light pink dress, and tan half inch heel shoes. After a day at the beach, Mom told me I could meet him. "Oh, no" I thought! "Not dressed like this!" I ran off to change. Running off to get ready, all I kept thinking was what would I do when I meet him. Do I bow, curtsey, shake his hand? What will he be wearing? In which room would I meet him? The ballroom oh, now that would be the perfect room! Would he be sitting on one of the little sofas by the grand piano and stand up as I entered and slightly bow to me? Oh, I could not wait and kept telling myself, "Linda, relax it is going to be just magical." As I came down the stairs, all dressed in my light pink dress with white pearls attached, I could hear Mom's voice in the butler's pantry. Was Mom talking to Dad and telling him my magical day was now going to happen? That is not Dad's voice. Could it the prince? "Please Mom don't say anything that would embarrass me" I thought. With my heart racing, slowly I entered the butler's pantry, and there he was with his back to me, leaning up against the table. Slowly turning around, he extended his hand to me. He took both my hands and he politely gave them a squeeze. He was all dressed in casual clothes, not dressed all in white or a robe and most of all no white turban. One thing I knew he would not be wearing - red pointy-toed shoes as in the movie Aladdin. Okay, I do think I watched too many movies or lived in a world of happy thoughts. I was a little disappointed that I did not meet him in the ballroom or morning room but it was a day I would always remember. He gave me his autograph, writing that he hoped I would make the long journey to his country to see him and put his address on the back. This is something I still have framed, along with a post card Miss Duke sent to my parents from India.

CHAPTER THIRTEEN

DOGS OF ROUGH POINT

While living at Rough Point, many dogs were also kept there. They each had a personality of their own. Shep was the only dog there for a few years. He was an old German Sheppard who could hardly get around. He was such a nice dog. Often he would sit on the back porch and wag his tail. He wagged his tail so hard it become flat on one side. I came home from school one day and was told he died. It was not until years later that I found out he was buried on the property. While Shep was still alive, Max came to the house from Duke Farms. We were told that someone on the farm had hit him while backing up a car. From this accident, he had a very bad back and was a very mean dog. All I know was he could not be trusted. Maybe he could sense we were afraid of him.

One afternoon someone was bitten quite badly. I came home from school and was told the person was on the property. Others said that the dog was off the property. Many phone calls were made back and forth to Duke Farms and the New York office about Miss Duke being sued. I was never told of the outcome. He also bit three of my own friends. My dad took two of them to the emergency room. One of the bitten friends was the son of a police officer. One girl was bitten on the leg while we were on the back lawn on one of the hills. The other girl was in the vegetable garden when she was bitten. Even I had two little nips on the leg. One was when I was walking up the driveway and the other was on the back porch. With so many being bitten in just a short time, a kennel was made for the dogs over by the vegetable garden. The dogs were only in it for a very short time.

My parents let me get a dog of my own. They got me a St. Bernard pup and I named her Daisy. A few years later, my dad got a Bulldog pup and Benny named him Poncho. We had orders to take care of them. I would often brush Daisy on the back porch. One-time Benny was outside playing with the dogs and he came running in saying that Poncho was hurt. He was hitting a baseball and hit the dog in the head. We all ran out the side door and got a surprise when we came back to the kitchen. Daisy had eaten one of the pies on the table and knocked the others on the floor. Miss Duke was coming up later that night. Mom did have time to make a couple more. I guess I was not watching her close enough. However, in my defense, it really was not my fault since my brother was the one who had us all go running out to check on Poncho. A very short time later Poncho was running and barking again. I do not recall them saying anything to him. No, it was, "Linda, you should have been watching Daisy." Oh well, the dog had great taste. She must have been thinking, I had better check this pie out to make sure it tastes as great as everyone says. I am still thinking now thank goodness it was not one of Miss Duke's dogs that got hurt and why couldn't it been one of the other dogs who ate the pie.

My job was to feed the dogs twice a day. I know this chore may seem like a small task to do but let me tell you that it was Not! Opening the cans on both ends (remember we did not have an electric can opener) was bad enough. It was mixing the raw eggs in with it. The smell was the worst part. I was told it was good for their fur. Then along came dry dog food shaped like burgers, just break apart and no smell. Not sure if touching the stuff was better but at least it did not smell. Was it true that once this kind of dog food was given to someone as a sandwich with ketchup? In addition, was a piece of dog candy eaten by mistake as a real chocolate candy? A few people out there must remember silly little things that happened among us. Looking back, it seems I have stories to tell of stories within stories. What can I say? My mind seems to run in many directions when thinking of things that happened at Rough Point.

Next would be dogs named Charlie and Henry. One dog was so shy that he would pick up his dog dish and walk off with it spilling as he went. Since he was in a way my boss, you know one of the masters of the house, I would have to clean it up and start all over getting him his food. In my defense, I could not understand why the five-second rule (you know the rule if it lands on the floor and it's less than five seconds it was good to eat) did not go for the dogs also. With all the complaining I did with the rule you would think I would just get the food and not say anything. The other dog would jump over the stone wall, and after a few times a high wire fence was put behind the wall. A few times when I was in high school my parents would spend the night at my Aunt Julia's home in Harwich, Massachusetts. I was not scared, maybe a little (who am I kidding, I was scared) I would let the three dogs out and Daisy would sleep in my room. By this time, people knew of the dogs living at Rough Point. With one extra big plus no one knew I was home alone.

Whenever Miss Duke would arrive, the dogs would have the run of the main house. The three dogs would be around her all the time. It was as if the dogs knew that they were in control and could go and do whatever they wanted. Many nights they would sleep in her bedroom and I am very sure it was on the bed or right outside the room.

In the fall of 1968, more dogs were to come from Duke Farms. Not sure how many more dogs came. All I remember was that it meant more cans, crumbling, eggs, and smell.

Looking back, I think that is why my children never had a dog. They would often ask, Mom, can we have a dog and a "BIG NO" would be the answer. Too much work. Do I feel guilty? "NO." Okay, maybe a little, but very, very little.

CHAPTER FOURTEEN

THE YEARS OF MY PARTIES

During the spring and winter of 1963 and 1964 were the years of the slumber parties on the fourth floor. My parents let my girlfriends and I have all the parties we wanted as long as we stayed on the fourth floor. At times, it would be only three girls and other times it would be twelve. Each knew what kind of snacks and records to bring along with their blankets and pillows. Two rooms were used so a few would get the beds. Others had the floor. Some would even sleep in the closet when using only one room. Before turning in for the night we would start a story and see who would be scared first. Making someone scared would at times be easy because you could hear the waves hitting against the rocks. On the other hand, was it the wind you could hear? Having the whole floor, we could run down the hallway, do cartwheels, and have pillow fights. One of the pillow fights landed me in the emergency room the next day with a dislocated shoulder. Then it would be who would fall asleep first. Usually, I was the first one to fall asleep. What was done while I was sleeping I would find out the next day. Did all these things really happen? Seeing ghosts or hearing strange noises coming from the main part of the house? And whose hand was put in cold water while sleeping? Did something happen or did they wake up before something did happen? Did anyone really leave the floor to check out what they thought they heard? On the other hand, is it lips are sealed as what really happens at Rough Point stays at Rough Point. As I remember, you can get to the main part of the house by the fourth floor. After cleaning up spilled popcorn and crumbs, we were off to the kitchen for toast and hot cocoa and making plans for the next party.

After graduating eighth grade, Mom and Dad said we could have a big party at the end of the summer. The party was held on the patio on the back lawn over by the solarium. With the lights on, the moon and stars overlooking the water, the place looked beautiful. It was a night any young woman could possibly dream of. The girls brought all the desserts, drinks and records. So many kids came from different age groups because some of my friends had older brothers and sisters already in high school. Some I am sure were eager to see what the estate looked like. The parents seemed more excited to be on the lawn when dropping off or picking up their children. It was a fun and amazing night for all. Everyone kept to the rule of staying on the patio.

It was not parties all the time. Friends would come just to hang out, either to do homework or make phone calls as with so many phones everyone could either listen or talk. Hanging out could mean being in the house for a while and then going down by the rocks and swimming under the bridge. Actually trying to swim, since your foot would get stuck in the seaweed. Once some of the girls and I found an outside door and discovered it was the coal shoot and thought it would be fun to slide down. We found out it was not the cleanest thing to do. Thank goodness we had washing machines. But the one big thing that did not go over with Mom was when we left the doors open all night. Thank goodness, no animals or strangers got in. Mom and

I were home alone that week. My dad had taken Benny to Philadelphia for his checkup.

One rainy Sunday night, four of my friends and I thought we would be brave and sleep in the solarium. We each chipped in money for our refreshments. It was an exciting night to sleep or try to sleep. The room was all windows and faced the back lawn. We could hear the waves crashing against the rocks. The next day was a different story. We forgot to get permission from Mom. (I am sure we did not really forget to ask, it was more like should we or should we not) and she had no idea where we were or what was the noise was coming from the solarium. I am almost sure no hot cocoa was served that morning. I seemed to remember a quick good bye to the girls.

I was entering high school that fall. It would mean meeting new friends. With new friends, it meant introducing myself and saying where I lived. Did some believe I was the caretaker's or maybe the owner's daughter? Okay, again, I watch movies and my favorite movie was *Sabrina*, staring Audrey Hepburn. (In this movie, she was the chauffer's daughter) After a few weeks, everyone knew who I was. It did maybe feel good for a while. On many Sunday afternoons, friends would gather at Rough Point. The boys would play football on the back lawn and the girls would watch. The number could be from five to as many of twenty- five. My parents then let us listen to records in the helps' dining room or we could go down to the basement, depending on the number of kids, and have soda and chips.

CHAPTER FIFTEEN

A BACK GATE

One day after school, I got a surprise! A gate was put up and it was locked. Did they forget about me I was thinking, or most likely, crying? How was I to get in? Do I walk down to Ledge Road that was a few blocks away and come around by the famous Cliff Walk? Cliff Walk is a three and half -mile walk overlooking the ocean with many of the famous mansions facing the cliff and then ending up at Bailey's Beach. On the other hand, do I climb over the fence and with a school uniform on that would be a little difficult? Luckily, for me, a friend's mom came by in a car and said when she got home she would call and tell someone I was at the gate. In the meantime, someone did come and let me in. Did they happen to remember I would be home soon or was it from the dogs barking so much? By the next day, an intercom system would be installed and I would be given a key.

A gate up meant no one could just stop by and come up to the house. So that was good, but with the gate meant many walks down to open it when someone came. My one friend remembers my dad going down twice or maybe even three times, to let her and another friend in and out. Did something strange happen that night at the gate to make them ring the bell so many times? Another time they came repeatedly, he finally told them to leave the key in the mailbox, and someone would pick it up later.

I am sure now the gate was meant for people to stay off the property and, more important, for keeping the dogs on the property to keep them safe and others too. Looking back, I recall when the gate was first installed the dogs could see the cars go by and within a few months a board was placed over the gate. Those passing by would not be able to see in but the dogs barking could be heard from a distance. As if warning people, "Please do not trespass or you will be in big trouble with us".

With the gate up it meant someone had to get out of the

car to open it. Each would look at each other to see who was going to open it. No big deal you are thinking but when you became the driver and the only one in the car or the only one who knew the dogs or should I say hope the dogs knew you. On those cold days to get out open the gate and then make sure none of the dogs would get out, drive into driveway, and get back out again closing the gate it became a big deal. Sometimes the driver would try to get someone to ride down with him and have him or her open the gate. In return, he would do the favor when asked. You can bet we kept count on whose turn it was next to open the gate for someone leaving or coming in.

CHAPTER SIXTEEN

SHE REALLY DID HAVE A KIND HEART

In the fall of 1964, my dad had a heart attack. He was on his way home from taking Miss Duke to the airport when he felt pain. He was in the hospital for a few weeks. When he finally did come home, the doctor gave strict him orders to rest and only come down the stairs once a day. Living on the third floor, it was rough for him to go up and down. We had a dumb waiter that went from the first to the third floor so we pulled him up and down as he sat in a chair. One day when I got home from school, I heard voices coming from our living room. What a surprise to see Miss Duke talking to my parents and giving my dad some books to read. She came in to Newport for the day. Later that night my mom told me that Miss Duke said we could move down to the second floor when Dad was up to it. That winter, Dad took time to get his health back in shape and planning his garden to be ready for the summer, and ready it was. During Dad's recuperation time Miss Duke often called to see how he was feeling. We also got our own phone number. Would Miss Duke be happy about the new phone line? I think so as times she would answer the phone. The buzzer would ring and the message would be "Tell Linda the babysitting time has been changed." I thought it was neat to tell someone you were talking to Miss Duke and not my mom.

During the Christmas break, we moved down to the second floor. Again, I got the room that overlooked the driveway. But I also had two windows, and the other overlooked the front lawn. This room was so much different from my other room. The room was painted by Mr. G as he once had this as his room. He painted the walls in a very light peach and very light purple, with built- in white shelves and a walk- in closet. The following Christmas I had a nice surprise. Dad had finished making my canopy bed. Mr. Tirella, who was a close friend of Miss Duke, had helped Dad make the bed. The bedposts were painted in white. The canopy was in white and gold material with the bedspread and drapes to match. I felt like a princess in the room. And peach has become another one of my favorite colors. I had a very tall beige armoire where I could place my two big stuffed animals and favorite pictures on top.

CHAPTER SEVENTEEN

LIVING ON THE SECOND FLOOR

Moving to the second floor would bring both sad and happy memories. Happy ones would be playing with my nieces when they would come up from New Jersey to visit. Lynn, my oldest niece who was three at the time would be waiting for me to come home from school. She would hide under the pillows on the sofa and would wait there until I found her even though her little feet would be sticking out.

One of the saddest memories was the autumn of 1966, the night of the terrible accident. I was up in my room when the phone rang. It was my friend Maggie and she was wondering what had happened at the house. I remember telling her that Miss Duke was here and she and her friend Mr. Tirella, were going out. She kept asking questions and more questions. And then she said something about the fence being knocked down. At that point, Maggie knew I had no idea what she was talking about. I could hear her mom in the background (saying something like maybe she does not know yet). I quickly got off the phone and went downstairs. I heard a lot of noise coming from the front of the house. In the kitchen the help were hugging each other and crying. My mom came over to me and told me about the accident and said Dad was down at the front gate. I walked down to the gate and heard noises. What a sight to see, the car across the street, the gate down, blood on the road, tire marks and so many people looking and shaking their heads and asking questions. Dad was standing there asking the people to step back. I was confused. The dogs were walking about and staying close to Dad. Did they sense something was wrong and needed to be with someone they trusted?

Even though when Miss Duke is at the house, the dogs didn't go near any of us, only to be fed. They were always by her side. Even my own St. Bernard dog, Daisy, was walking with the other dogs. Daisy hardly ever went on the front lawn. The next day was Saturday and I was a sophomore in an all-girls Catholic high school. That usually meant meeting up with girlfriends, talking about boys, football game, eating hot dogs and more talking of boys. Mom and Dad thought it would be good for me to be with friends. Dad had been talking with employees at Duke Farms and later that night, he came to me and said it would be best if I didn't go as people may ask questions that I could not answer properly. Early evening on Saturday, my friend Patty called and said that many people, both kids and adults came to her and asked if my father was okay. Many believed it was my dad who got killed that night since he usually unlocked the gate. My mom was even sent flower arrangements. The next few days you would find many people coming and going. Police officers, doctor, and lawyers came in from New York and even some of Miss Duke's closest friends. Many would walk or drive by to try and get a look at the broken, twisted gates and Dad would ask them to leave. He would be asked how she was and he would simply say she is resting and would not give his name if asked and Daisy would be by his side. Living on the second floor, we were separated from the main house by a short hallway, a few stairs and a door that did not block out the sounds of Miss Duke crying. The next few weeks would be rough on all of us. I remember walking uptown with some of my girlfriends and hearing boys from the nearby boys' high school calling out saying, "There is the girl who lives at the murderer's house." "No, it was an accident," I screamed. "No," they would yell "that was no accident, he was murdered." My girlfriends let me cry and talk of the night. I told them that. Mr. Tirella got out of the car to open the gates. There was not enough room as the gates opened inward. Instead of getting back in the car, Miss Duke slid over to the driver's side and stepped on the gas pedal; she thought the car was in reverse. I came home crying and telling my mom and Mrs. Veary (a very close friend who often came with Miss Duke) what had happened. Mrs. Veary took me aside and we talked. I even now still think she was reading my mind; I wanted to ask if I could see Miss Duke. She assured me that Miss Duke was okay. It was a sad and difficult time right now she said, but that in time things would be okay. Later that week she came to my room with a gift. It was a light color green stone bracelet which I still have now.

What was the public really thinking? Did they really think it was not an accident? How could anyone mistake a gas pedal for the brake and step so hard that it knocked down a fifteen-foot iron gate and went straight across the street straight into a tree? Did they really think she got off without a punishment? Was anyone offered a payoff? Did she start a new project in town? To some it was, yes. Each of us will have our own thoughts of what happened that night.

Who was the man who was killed on that Friday night? To me, He was a gentle kind man who would be missed by many. No more hearing him whistle as he would arrange the flowers, see his big smile or hear his soft voice, see his wave as he would walk by the kitchen. Often I went with Dad to take Mr. Tirella to the airport. Sometimes, it would be to Providence and he would talk of the different projects he had worked on over the years. Being an interior designer, he had many stories to tell of whom he met.

The house was closed with the sheets covering everything. Little was said of Mr. Tirella after that fall. His room the beautiful red velvet room (the same room Miss Duke had as a little girl) with the gorgeous canopy bed was never slept in after that horrible night. By Christmas, the many of the newspapers had stopped covering the story. The whispers and pointing faded away. It seemed like a long, cold winter. My dad was sick a few times that winter with his heart and was in the hospital. We also had a family death in Canada.

CHAPTER EIGHTEEN

A NEW YEAR

Spring came and I would find Dad working in the garden. Mom would be working in the main part of the house. That summer Miss Duke was not up much. We had family members come and visit from Canada, Massachusetts and New Jersey.

During the fall of 1967, Miss Duke would often say on Monday she would be up on Friday with a few friends and then Mrs. Veary would call and say" No" they would be staying at the farm maybe next week. Again, it seemed it would be a long fall and winter.

Other accidents also happened at the back gate that fall. Rough Point was at the bend of Bellevue Avenue. It was hard to see the wall on foggy nights. Because of this, I would hear a car hitting the wall and the back gate bell would ring. Dad would go and say he had already called the police. Phone calls back and forth to Duke Farms and then to the mason for him to come and give estimates to have the wall fixed. I know it's hard to believe that someone could miss seeing a brick wall.

CHAPTER NINETEEN

A YEAR OF CHANGE

In February of 1968, Miss Duke came to Newport with a few people. Miss Duke asked my Dad to take herself and her guests out to dinner. The dinner meeting must have gone well because that spring Dad had extra help in the flower and vegetable gardens.

All the summer help came back from New Jersey and New York. Mrs. G also came back as a cook. I had never met her before but had heard a lot about her. Her bedroom was on the second floor with her own private bathroom just as she had many years before. She was a Swedish cook and an excellent cook she was. She was much older than any of the other cooks who had worked here.

Mrs. G was so different from the first summer cook,

Mrs. D. Mrs. D had come from the South and her way of cooking was so much different. She had her southern charm and made the best fried chicken and peach cobbler. That summer I had my driver's license so one of my jobs was to take Mrs. G grocery shopping. At times, my best friend Sheila came with us. She would often let us buy some snacks and a few times bought Sheila a carton of cigarettes. Once we asked her if we could have a bag of chips and she said she would make them. They were so good but a bag would have been a lot quicker. Since I had my license, I would often go with Dad to pick Miss Duke up at the airport. I would take the luggage and Dad took Miss Duke. This would be one of the few times I could use the front gate.

  Later that summer Miss Duke's nephew Walker came up with one of his school friend's. I thought he would be dressed in khaki color slacks and button solid color shirt. No! It was a purple and green polka dot shirt, jeans and a pair of beach sandals. Not the kind of clothes a millionaire would wear, I thought. Sheila and I offered to take him uptown to help him buy some new clothes. He said yes, but we never ended up doing it. Wonder if he thought we were thinking of ourselves when talking of shopping. After all, we were girls and that's what girls like to do, shop. Using someone else's money seemed to be fun. He did not seem to care when I told him that his toys were stored on the fourth floor all these years, and that I had wanted to play with some of the board games.

One weekend when Walker and his friend came up they had a gentleman with them and he was to watch the activities they did. Before taking the boys out for the night he came into the kitchen and offered me some wine "No thank you," I said politely and he insisted a few more times. The last time he grabbed my face and put the glass to my mouth with that I pushed his hand and said a teary "NO". He left the kitchen in a rush and I went upstairs to my room. Later that night I was called to come to the kitchen. Miss Duke and the man were waiting for me and I accepted his apology. One of the maids informed Miss Duke and my parents what had happened. That was the last time I saw him come to Newport.

One other night, Walker and his friend went up town and met some girls and proceeded to tell them who he was and where he lived. They asked the girls if they would like to come to the house the next day for breakfast. The girls informed them that they had been there before and said no thanks. The next day he asked me about them and I said "Oh yes one went to Saint Catherine's (the high school where I went) and yes they have been here. He was not happy that others had been to the house. We had a few choice words and later that day we were both called to the kitchen. We both were told that this was my home to have friends over at my part of the house and his friends in his part of the house. So we went our separate ways and did not talk much after that.

The summer of 1968 went fast. Soon it would be time to go back to school. Miss Duke and Mrs. Veary stayed until after the middle of October. The reason I remember October, was because on the 16th of that month we would be moving back to New Jersey. I was at Sheila my best friend's house when Dad called and asked me to come home, as he needed to tell me something. By the sound of his voice, I knew something was wrong. Going into the house, I saw some of my items being taken out and being put in the dumpster. The two items that stand out in my mind even now are my two big dolls. I'm not sure what happened to my bike, because I am sure no one got the bike. My mom had been sick a few times that summer and it was suggested that we move and live at Duke Farms. Dad was not sure when we would be moving only that it would be within the next few weeks. I knew deep down it would be good for my mom to move, but all I could think it was my senior year and I was not going to like moving away. Did my parents realize how hard I had to study that summer to pass my test to become a citizen of the United States? I had gone to the court house with my two sponsors and passed the test and now I just had to wait for the date to be sworn in. How each day I would look in the mail to see if I got the paperwork explaining how to join the Peace Corps when I finished high school and how happy I was when all the paperwork came that day in September. How upset I was for those few weeks and just wanted someone to let me stay with them (even though I knew how homesick I would be away from my parents. I was going to make a point to let everyone know how upset I was with this move). One friend's mom did say I could stay with them to finish the year. How excited I was when I told my dad that I found someone to stay with and was not expecting the answer to be no. No, why would he say no? He politely reminded me the reason. May of that same year I dented the door of the driver's side of my friend's car when I backed into her. When we left the scene and went to her house, her stepfather was waiting for us at the door and not very happy. For a few weeks she was without a car and I was grounded for a few weeks from using my dad's car for school. (Plus I had to pay for the accident with babysitting money I made). And to me that meant walking the forty-five minutes home from school. So, I had no choice but to agree with him, even though I really wanted to stay in Newport. So again, it was good-bye to old friends and hoping to meet new ones. It was a sad day for Mom that Saturday saying good- bye to the help at Rough Point. The staff was waiting for her in the hallway with each giving her a hug, kisses and whispering something in her ear. My dad would come back on Monday to take my brother and me down on Wednesday. With my parents being away for the weekend that meant I could stay out late or at least I thought it would be a nice idea. The staff was given orders by my dad that I had to be in by eleven and not a minute later. So yes, the side door would come in handy that weekend or at least I thought it would. To my surprise yes, Mrs. G was waiting for me that Saturday night as I came in at midnight. In her sweet Swedish accent shaking her head and pointing her finger she gave her lecture about being late. She did promise not tell my dad on Monday and kept the promise. At least I think she did. The last few days of school were sad, saying good-bye to some close friends and having my picture taken out in front of the school with some of them. My new school would it be small like St. Catherine's? We had less than three hundred girls, and our graduating class was less than sixty. We had one priest to teach religion to the junior and seniors, one lay teacher, eight nuns for teachers, and one nun for a principal. Yes, St Catherine's was a small school and one I liked very much with close friends in each grade. Would I keep close contact with them or would Newport be a thing of the past, a time to forget and start new all over again. Only time would tell what would happen.

CHAPTER TWENTY

BEHIND THE IRON GATES OF DUKE FARMS

Moving to Duke Farms meant that this would be the first time seeing what was behind the big iron gates. We pulled up to the guardhouse, we said our names and the gates were opened and we drove in. Funny, isn't this how it all started back in 1961? Giving names and a gate opens. Many questions go through my mind. Would our home be like Rough Point, but be surrounded by trees and not water? How many other families would be here? Would the atmosphere be the same when Miss Duke arrives? Soon some of my questions were answered. The farm is really a farm with over two thousand acres and had many houses on the property. Only this time we did not get to live in the big house.

The house we did live in was called the Boathouse. It

was right by the pond with the ducks and swans. One important lesson to learn was to make sure the glass doors were closed tightly unless you want to wake up to a duck in your room. It was a stone house and only had four rooms. The living room was big enough so that a table would fit, where we were able to sit and eat. That was good since the kitchen was so small it only had just enough room for one or two people. A fireplace built from stone was in the living room and we did get our use from it. The two bedrooms were rather large. We were able divide one room into two. A lot different from the house I had once lived in. In the back of the house was all woods and a little wooden bridge. The main house was not that far away. On the property were other little houses that families lived in who worked at the farm. The greenhouses there were famous. People would come and view them but I never had the chance to see. I have heard about them from many people.

    The new school was so much different from St. Catherine's. My parents had told me I could go to a Catholic School. We went to enroll me and let's say I did not go as I had no transcript or letter saying I was a senior. Sister Elizabeth Thomas (the senior advisor who also taught shorthand and typing) told me when I knew what school I was going to, to have the school send a letter and transcripts would be sent out right away. We left the school and I told my parents that I would go to the public school with Benny. I could see the relief in my dad's eye as going to the public school meant no tuition costs, paying for books, and no costs for uniforms. Somerville High School was so big and overcrowded that they had triple sessions. I was in the third session. The bus would pick us up at the gate. I was not happy but knew I only had one year left and I could move back to Newport. Or so I thought. The school counselor knew I was unhappy about going to such a big school and made a suggestion that I go to the Vocational School and work in the afternoon. Monday, November fourth my dad took me to the school and I could start the following week. In New Jersey many of the schools were closed for Election Day and on Thursday and Friday they are closed for teacher's convention. (Many schools are still closed for the Election Day and on Thursday and Friday of that week schools are closed for teachers' convention.) Since school was closed for the week, my parents said I could take a bus to Newport. I think they believed I would come back with a different attitude for school and deep down maybe I thought I would. I left early on Tuesday to catch the bus for New York and arrive in Newport early evening. My friend Sheila and another friend picked me up at the bus stop. Sheila's dad was my dad's best friend. Wednesday, Thursday, and Friday I went to school with Sheila. I was able to get a letter from Sister Elizabeth Thomas saying I was a senior. Sister stated she got a letter from the Catholic School and after she sent out my transcripts she got another letter, I then proceeded to tell her she would be getting another letter. She asked why I did not go to the Catholic School and when I told her I had no way of proving I was a senior, she said she was sorry that she did not think of writing a letter for me. Friday night came and I went out with many friends and which meant getting in late. This did not go over great with Sheila's parents. Saturday morning would mean a lecture; of that I was sure. Before coming downstairs, Sheila said I had a phone call. I picked up the phone and I could hear my sister Audrey talking but could not figure out what she was saying to me. She kept saying so are you leaving today and I would say no, on Monday, Mom and Dad said I could stay until Monday. Sheila's mom said "Linda does not know anything". Upon hearing my sister said she was sorry for raising her voice and told me that dad was taken to the hospital with a heart attack. I asked through my tears how bad and how was Mom. Mom was doing okay and she was not sure if dad would make it. Sheila walked me to the bus stop; we gave each other a hug and I told her I would call when I got home to Duke Farms.

    Many family members were at the house even Mom, who was resting at the time. I did get to hear more about Dad's condition. My cousin said the doctors were not sure how much longer he would live but were surprised he was lasting this long. I kept thinking that was a good sign. Dad told Mom he wanted to see his children, eight brothers and one sister from Canada. Phone calls were made to Dad's brothers keeping them posted on his conditions. They would be down as soon as my one uncle from Quebec arrived. I went with Mom and others to see him and he did wake and held my hand. On Sunday, other family members came to the house and would take my mom (she did not have a driver's license) to the hospital. I did go with her and my brother- in- law one time. Dad rested and did not know I came to visit. Monday night evening came and the drive to the hospital seemed so different and even the chill in the air seemed to be different. Mom seemed different as if she knew something was going to happen on that cold November night. When we got on the elevator a man politely asked what floor and who we were visiting. The asking of so many questions was a little different from the other times we came to visit. When we got off our floor he asked us to wait in a room telling us they were having problems with lights on this floor. A nurse came into the room and informed us that dad had passed away, within the last half hour as we were on our way to the hospital. My two sisters, brother in law and myself looked at Mom to see her reaction. How calm she was. My sister Nita was pregnant with her first child, crying and shaking. Mom quickly went to her putting her arms around her and told her sit down. I often thought how proud Dad would have been of her; how she kept the family together. All I could think what was Mom going to do without Dad? We had only lived in New Jersey for three weeks how could this have happened so quickly and was my life going to change? Benny had stayed at home with my older cousin Larry. My uncles from Canada did not get to see Dad before he died.my uncles brought with them the Canadian flag to drape over his coffin. My dad's sister was too sick with cancer to make the trip. Mom's sisters and my grandmother came down from Canada also. Flowers were sent from Miss Duke, Duke Farms and Rough Point employees. I guess it was fate that mom was now living so close to her two sisters, two daughters and two grandchildren. Mom, my brother, and I lived at the farm until that December. My sister Audrey asked my mom if she would like to live with her and her two children. I am sure it was a difficult decision for her to make. A decision she knew would affect family members and her. After all, she was living in a new place, not feeling well and without my dad. She felt she was alone. She thought moving was doing the best thing for everyone. What would this new move mean to me? Another school I and did not even get a chance to go to the vo-tech school and so I told mom I was not going to go to school I was quitting and would go to night school or just get my GED. And I did. It would take another year but I got my GED. A few days before we were to move I received a letter in the mail that I would be sworn in as a citizen. Mr. Dugan (my Dad's closet friend and one of my sponsors) went to the court house and explained that we had moved, so a new letter was written and they would inform me when I would be able to take a new test. Again, a new letter was written stating I had taken the test and past. I received another letter stating that in the near future I would get sworn in. Benny went to live with my aunt and uncle who had boys close to his age. Mom and I moved in with my sister and her two little girls about a half an hour away from him.

CHAPTER TWENTY-ONE

A NEW BEGINNING

The winter months would go by fast. I got a job working as a file clerk at a company, where my cousin Stella also worked. In January, my cousin Larry enlisted in the Air Force and the family gave him a going away party. We had a baby shower for Nita in February. Waiting and wondering when the new little one would arrive. Plus, I was going to be godmother. This made for more anticipation of the new arrival. Another happy event was my cousin Stella was getting married and asked me to be her maid of honor. Dress fittings, planning for showers gift buying and all the excitement that went with a wedding helped to ease my sadness. Stella's wedding would mean relatives would be coming from Canada and Alabama. Stella's wedding and Nita's, baby's birth would take place in April and, in fact, a week apart from each other. My cousin would be married on the fifth of

April. Nancy my, goddaughter, would be born a little after midnight on the twelfth. All was not joyful for our family. My grandmother came from Canada for Stella's wedding and had a heart attack a few days later. She passed away the same day Nancy was born. I felt bad for Mom as she was going to Canada with other family members to bury her mother. This would be her first trip to Canada without my dad. When Mom came back from Canada she moved in with Nita to help with the baby. Nancy's christening would be in May.

By the third week in May, Mom was not herself. At times all she wanted to do was stay in bed and then her smile changed. Her mouth started to droop to one side and her walk was slow. My sister Audrey and my Aunt Stella took her to the hospital on that Wednesday night with signs we thought were of a stroke. After a few tests, it turned out she had a brain tumor. She would often say she had a headache and would often take extra aspirins. We found out on Friday night how sick she really was.

She was to be operated on Monday but sadly, on Saturday night she went in a coma and died four days later. Mom died on June eleventh exactly seven months to the day dad died. The days leading up to her death was so painful to see her laying there, so still and not knowing how sick she was for those years. The nurses would tell me I could touch her and talk to her. How angry I was at her for leaving me, how could she do this? She was in pain for so many years and now a new doctor was going to make her better. Why didn't she hang on for those few days and she would be her old self again? How could she do this to me? The day of her funeral walking up to the coffin saying my last good bye to her, it was then that I held her in my arms and gave her my last good bye kiss. Her death would leave an impact on me for many years. Some I know were for selfish reasons. She was not there for the births of my children. She was alive when my nieces were born. She also went to the hospital all those times with my brother. Mom's friend Mary often said Dad could not do anything without Mom, and he was calling her to be with him. Mom's two sisters and one brother came down from Canada along with two of my dad's brothers. My sister Audrey called Duke Farms and then wrote to Miss Duke telling her how sick Mom was while she had been working for her in Newport. After her death, I stayed with my sister Audrey and her two little girls. Benny moved to my sister Nita's house, who lived forty-five minutes away. I could go once a week to have dinner with him and go again on weekends to visit with him.

CHAPTER TWENTY-TWO

GOING BACK

Did I ever go back to Duke Farm? Yes, a year later I went back to see some of the maids. Did I ever go back to Rough Point? Yes, but it was years and years later. It took me a long time to even drive by Rough Point when I would go visit friends in Newport. In 1970, I sent Miss Duke my wedding announcement but never heard from her. I read of Miss Duke's death (October 28, 1993) in the paper. *People* magazine had an article about her and so I sent a letter to editors of *People* magazines saying how I had known her.

I read in the paper that Rough Point was going to be open to the public. In the summer of 2000, my husband and I were going to Newport for a visit. I decided to call the Newport Restoration Foundation (the Foundation Miss Duke had founded) and tell them who I was and asked if we could get a tour of Rough Point and would it be possible to see the helps' quarters. We went to the office with pictures I have of Rough Point. A woman from the office took us to the house. We were given a private tour by two people, a woman from the office and gentleman who worked at the house. Would going through the house bring back any memories? Would any of the rooms look the same and have the same items as I remembered? We did a lot of talking on our tour. I told the people of how some of the items were usually placed on this piece of furniture or that piece of furniture. Miss Dukes' bedroom was slightly different. The purple walls were gone. The walls now are yellow but still in purple accents, the gold hairbrush still there and all the mother-of-pearl furniture. Miss Duke's canopy bed had been replaced by another canopy bed as my dad had helped Mr. Tirella make the other one. I was hoping that the green lime swimsuit cover up would be there. I remember the time Mom let me try it on and then I spilled homemade hot fudge on it. It was the first and last time she ever let me try on one of Miss Duke's outfits. Nevertheless, I sure did love having it on for those few brief moments. Going into Mr. Duke's room, it still gave me that cold feeling but the bathroom was off limits. I told them of the scale being built into the floor. And I showed a picture of a bed that once was there. Now the room was to become a museum of Miss Duke's items. Seeing the solarium was different .no tall geraniums were there. (Even now the smells of geraniums bring me back to memories of this room.) Seeing the pictures of camels that once roamed the place after I moved was such a surprise. Other rooms brought back memories as Mr. Tirella's room was where my girlfriend, Maureen Dugan West, and I slept. The room still had the canopy bed with soft red velvet walls. That time we did have permission to sleep there. It was the room my uncle once slept one winter night and woke up with a bad headache from the smell of the mothballs. I remembered wondering who would get to sleep in this room- a very special person he was.

    Many of the other rooms looked the same. The Great Hall with high ceilings still has flags hanging down. The tapestries are still hanging on the walls. As a child I would think why would anyone hang a rug on a wall? In addition, yes, the yellow room or hallway still painted in light yellow and white trim. With the sunlight, shining in on the chandeliers I could see the colors dancing on the walls. Just like the one in the Pollyanna movie starring Haley Mills when she and her little friend with the help from a kind old man had the prism all strung up on a line? Not that anyone tried to do that. Maybe in a way I am like the "Glad Girl "with many different memories of a home that was once lived in by some regular folks.

To some people the ballroom was a formal room, (now it is called the Music Room) but to me, it was the room where we had our last family picture taken December 25th, 1967. Mrs. Veary's room with the mother- of- pearl bed, the bedroom with the little stairways to the bathroom is now an office. The music room with the hidden closet in the panel walls is now called the pine room. We were then taken to the fourth floor by way of the main part. Funny that is how we were taken the night we moved in. The rooms are now offices. To me it was the floor of the slumber parties of 1964 and 1965. Yes, those were the days. I asked to see the second floor helps' side and the third floor. We did get to see the second floor. My bedroom of peach and purple is now an office. The only floor we did not get to see was the third floor as the new caretakers lived there. To me, they were the new family, even though they had lived there for years. Would they have the same kind of memories I have of the summer cottage.

We were then taken to the kitchen where many memories rushed through my mind. One special one was of the violets I would pick on my way home from school and Mom would place them in a small vase right next to the flowers from the garden. How proud I was of my small bouquet next to the garden ones. And remembering the different summer help who once have worked here. For examples the maid with the red hair and the one with the gold tooth. The one man who would put orange juice in his cereal instead of milk. He would say he did not like the taste of milk and was getting his fruit for the day. Many things were still the same and yes the same black and white tiles. The copper pots hanging down from the ceiling (could they be the same ones my dad took down to the basement to shine and polish with his own sander to make them glow) over the table where playing cards would slip in between the slots.

The stove changed some. It was still black, but part of it was gone and a fireplace was behind one part of it. Wow, that would have been something to have in the kitchen years before for making popcorn during one of the slumber parties. One of the old fashion iceboxes replaced the white refrigerator we had. The vegetable room was gone too. The maid's pantry was next. When I entered the room the one thought came back and that would be opening all the cans of dog food. Turning around I got a big surprise! On the table were ice cream sundaes ready to enjoy. Tears began to form! I felt like the lady of the house this time. All I could remember was this was my kitchen, where friends came to eat and play. A room Miss Duke would often come to sit, talk, and eat a light meal after swimming off the rocks. My nieces would play and one would have a bath in a basin (how many children can say that their mom was bathed on a table at Rough Point?)

    I then asked about the basement. I mentioned the pullout dryers. It seemed they had been replaced, since they had, no idea of what I was talking about (could not wait to tell my sister because she would hang my niece's diapers in there and they would be so stiff.) The same spins machine where I would ring out my sweaters. We went to the far end of the basement, which now has an indoor swimming pool, something I always wanted. Looking back, best it was not in when my friends came over.

Off to the lawn where the dogs had roamed. A smile came to my face as I remember the time Benny and I were playing croquette and with one fast hit and bang the cellar window broke. My dad calling down or most likely yelling with all this property you manage to break a window. All the ground men were busy working. Wow! My dad had himself and one other person to do the mowing and weeding (except the last two summers he had an extra person and one was my brother) Walking around the grounds hearing strangers telling me stories of Rough Point all seemed so unreal to me. I asked many questions of the different people who had once worked there, telling them stories of some. The man who on his first day of work helped my dad cut the hedges that sent dad to hospital for a couple of stitches.

Seeing tourists walking the grounds, all I kept thinking was this was my house, my house where friends came to play and family members came to visit. We even got dressed in our finest to have our pictures taken in the ballroom. Benches now have been placed on the back lawn so you can sit and take in the view of the house and water. The front lawn was the same, the circular driveway where I learned how to drive. The driveway was still filled with small stones. Still standing were the few big trees in the middle of the lawn where the dogs would often rest underneath and where I asked my dad if I could have a tree swing and a big "No" would be his answer. Looking back, I can see now why No was so often my parents' answer. You cannot say I did not try.

We were off to the garden and, yes, the roses still form an arch. While going in the garden, many memories came back of seeing Dad working- either planting or weeding, and me thinking this is where I always wanted to have my wedding someday. It would have been a perfect place, with roses to walk under, to meet your special mate at the end of the aisle, the ocean behind you, and all the flowers you could imagine to make a perfectly wonderful day. Even a carriage ride from the front doors, can't you just picture it- a walk down the main staircase with the sunlight shining in the windows, with the coat of arms with a twenty-foot train flowing over the marble floor and then off to the garden. A dream, I know, but the thought has stayed with me all these years. I did ask a few years later if my youngest daughter Jillian could have her wedding here and was told no, that they do not have public events here. I have granddaughters now and maybe one day one of theirs will be there. On the other hand, maybe a renewal of my wedding vows. You never know what can happen in years to come. Doug and I had our picture taken in the garden over by the same white statue and another one with one of the dogs.

Four more times I have come back to Rough Point. The next time it was 2002 with my sister Audrey, her daughter Lynn and Lynn's son Ryan who was eight. Two of my four children came also. We were again given a private tour. The first floor on the servant's side was closed off to the public as they were renovated. (My sister was a little disappointed) to our family the helps side was where we have our memories I know tourists cannot wait to see where the famous Poorest Rich Girl Lived.

Sitting outside on the benches my nephew Ryan said, "Aunt Linda, I like this place. Can you move here and I can come and visit you?" I thought yes I lived here but it was not my house. I can remember these words being said to me many years before. Thinking again yes it would be nice to live here again. I would be the tour guide, but I am sure if you were on my tour you would not learn who did the great paintings. Mine would be here is where Mr. or Mrs. stayed, or guess who came from where and did what. Maybe I should not be the guide.

The third time I went back was the summer of 2004. Doug and I again were also given a private tour and with this tour, we were given the opportunity to see the help's dining room. This special room brings back so many memories as where we would have our Christmas tree in the corner. Dad would tie a rope around the tree to keep it standing up. At times having three big dogs, wagging their tails and each trying to see who could get under the tree first. Glass ornaments would come falling off the tree and I hoped that none broke. Our last Christmas was a memory in itself. My nieces would be spending it with us along with their mom and my other sister and her husband. My niece Lynn still talks of the gifts being mixed up where we got each other's gift. Now what would I do with a children's book of stories? Was not that the Christmas I was to get a new charm for my bracelet? Mom would often hide our wrapped Christmas gifts under one of the covered tables in the dining room and it was never found. On the other hand, as I like to think, someone found it and have him or her thinking did this charm belong to Miss Duke? I really do like to dream. The dining room was where our family would do jigsaw puzzles and my sister Nita loved lighting the fireplace. Hearing certain songs can remind me of the albums that I borrowed of Miss Duke's and somehow forgot to return them. I still do have one. Songs the house cleaners would hum as they worked in the kitchen. I have the picture of my sister, Mom and me sitting on the back porch as we watched my nieces busy washing Pappy's truck. (Pappy was what they called my dad) It was Miss Duke's truck but they thought it was Pappy's. My sister Nita and I having our pictures taken with the dogs by a stranger, who would become a close friend. She and her friend came from Connecticut to visit Newport one spring and found my dad and his helper out front raking. They asked if they could visit the grounds and they came back each spring to say hi.

When I ask family members what comes to their mind first when they hear Doris Duke or Rough Point, each of them will have their own special memory. One remembers my father being asked by Miss Duke to take her to the drive in." Why the drive in," I asked my cousin Stella. "Why did you say that with all the other things you could have said?" She said, "That is what stands out in my mind." Did they really go to the drive in you are thinking and the answer will be your own guess? However, I do remember the time Dad being teased the time he took her and a few guests to the movies. Was it because of being asked or the name of the movie? I always like to compare it to Daddy War bucks buying out the whole theater as he did for Annie. Again another movie I compare Rough Point to. My cousin Sharon remembers my mom being asked by Miss Duke to pick up her feet when she walked, as this is "No Hash House" she was told. My parents missing Sharon's wedding in New Jersey as Miss Duke and guests happen to come up that weekend and they could not get away. Others remember playing on the lawn or jumping on and off the rocks. Playing cards at the kitchen table and having the cards fall between the cracks of the table. The copper pots and pans hanging down in the middle of the table and let's not forget trying to get a sneak glimpse of Miss Duke. My younger cousin Peter and his older brother Larry say dogs and they even remember the name of the dog that bit people. Peter often shows his friends the postcard I sent him of Rough Point and tells them this is where my cousins lived and where I would go for family vacations. Did they believe him? Only he knows the answer. The pies mom made were said by many. The lemon meringue pie with mountain top peaks even with the occasional lemon seed was so delicious. Yet others remember her apple pies not being as delicate but just as delicious. The gardens were said by many remembering the arch of the roses, the deep colors of purple of the Gerbera daisies, soft pastel colors of the gladiolas and the dinner plate size dahlias. A smile and a tear come to many but each remembers a cottage that was a castle to a little girl named Linda.

  Friends will tell you of coming to play, having snacks,

and using all the phones. Even one former classmate said at a class reunion that he could not believe the items in the house were worth so much, until his daughter became a tour guide at another mansion and told him the value of some of the antiques. He said "Linda, we had fun at Rough Point playing football on the back lawn, listening to records in the basement and just hanging with friends." It was such a nice talk I had with him remembering his time at the summer cottage and even mentioning my parents. A few even remember a night when we were in eighth grade. It was to be a fun night of pizza and soda. Then a turn of events happened Miss Duke came up unexpected. Now what were we to do? Dad said we could use a certain part of the back lawn. It was a night of heating up pizza, bringing it out on the lawn, and peeking over the hedges to see Miss Duke and a friend swim off the rocks. At one point, she gave us a wave. A few remember the night someone was thrown in a neighbor's pool and got someone's blazer ruined. Do two of them remember Mom and Dad letting us watch the Wizard of Oz in Mr. Dukes' room as it was the only room with a color television? I wonder what others would remember if they went back to revisit. My one friend and I remember the time my parents were away and we were going to take the truck out. Neither one of us knew how to drive a stick but she had brothers who did. When her one brother was dropping her off she asked him questions of how to drive a stick. With going forward instead or reverse we decided to stop. Now where we were going to go we did not know but we had fun thinking of what we were going to do. She did learn how to drive a stick and I never did and my two older children can vouch for that.

Others will say they often have over heard tourists say they can hardly wait to see the house and the clothes she wore. They smile and say they have slept there and even touched her clothes. Living in New Jersey I hear the senior citizens say they are going on a bus tour to see the gardens at Duke Farms. I smile and say I lived there.

My sister Audrey did go back to visit Rough Point with her daughter Dawne and granddaughter Marissa. With this visit she got to see the kitchen. Marissa can now say that's the table where her mom was bathed.

The fourth time I came to visit was the fall of 2008 with two close friends. One was a friend I met when I first moved to Newport in 1961 and the other a friend I met in high school. Maybe this was a visit I seemed to enjoy in a different kind of way. My friend Claire who often came to play and, with Barb who had never been to Rough Point. Seeing the expressions on their faces as our tour guide explained the pieces. We each took turns asking questions. I guess with growing older you learn to appreciate the paintings or really the portraits that are done by Thomas Gainsborough. And finding out how valuable some of the items are. Plus, the value of those that are no longer there. We learned that the wallpaper in the ballroom are of two different designs but are similar to color and style. All I thought it was paper with birds in trees. The big clock is in Louis XVI style built of carved and gilded wood. To us it was a big gold clock that looked like the sun. The Sleeping Baby was even still there. Funny I just thought of it as the little baby everyone was asked to touch as they passed by. Not sure if the tour guide could picture servants touching the Sleeping Baby. We were told the history of the artist.

The Great Hall, we learned so many interesting things. The room is approximately the same size as it was when built. Mr. and Mrs. Duke did raise the ceiling and replaced the dark wood floor with marble. The tapestries, how each one told a story and they were told in three panels; for example, the wedding story. Funny how each time I saw them it was oh look at those rugs hanging and why, never looking at them as telling a story. The two three- legged side tables were still there one on each of the fireplace. My mom would say how much she loved them. "So small but they seemed to be so special, she would say." A few items were gone. One was the fifty-cent rug. The rug looked well-worn in the 60's and even then no one was allowed to step on it. We even had the opportunity to watch as a woman was mending one of the beautiful tapestries.

In front of Miss Duke's room, the row of lights is no longer there. The complete second floor of bedrooms on the servant's side, now had items that belonged to Miss Duke that had special meanings to her, for example her animals. We were able to watch movie clips of Miss Duke playing with her dogs.

Our tour ended with going downstairs to the servant's side. Claire was remembering drinking the hot cocoa after the slumber parties or just enjoying friends laughing and maybe crying. When we left on that rainy day, you can be sure I did ask about a missing charm. The tour guide laughed and reassured me that if a charm was found she would keep me in mind. Still, I like to think it was found and someone is thinking that they have found a piece of Miss Duke's belongings. The only floor that I still have not been on since leaving Rough Point is the third floor. Looking up at the three windows where my bedroom was for so many years, the radiator where my brother hit his head and has a scar over his eyebrow from it. The gardens were getting ready to be closed. Gone were the pinks, bright yellows, bold purples, sunset oranges and the reds of the roses.

    Even though I had moved away so many years before when something was in the news concerning Miss Duke someone would call and say did you hear this about Miss Duke. That would bring the memories of when the Restoration Society was being formed where Miss Duke was fixing up older homes in Newport. I had no idea what kids would be talking about back in 1968. With fixing up the homes people were moving out of they would say something like, "members of my family have nowhere to live. Thank your father's boss." It was like I had something or my family had something to do with it. Not until I would visit Rough Point and read of what Miss Duke did of fixing up the homes bringing them back to the look of the 1800's did I know what they were speaking about.

The fifth time I came back was the summer of 2010 and that visit is one I will treasure forever. My grandson, Justin, who was seven and half was on the tour with me (his little sister of nine months started out with us along with their mom but Madelynn was getting loud and their mom took her out so the other guest could enjoy the tour). Watching his eyes beam with excitement as we entered the rooms, I was thinking to myself "what is he thinking"? The tour guide knew I had once lived there. She was telling a story about the servant's quarters and said something like" Would you know if this is true and if so how would you know?" I had eyes looking at me as my answer would be yes it is true as I lived here for seven and half years. She then asked what floor I lived on. I explained that we started out living on the third floor and my dad had a heart attack and we moved to the second floor. She then explained that the second floor was now part of the tour and that my bedroom was no longer there. As the guide is explaining my grandson is giving my arm a tug and whispered in my ear "Grammy you don't have a bedroom to go to when you come back here". I am not sure if he thought that we were going to stay there for the night but it was so cute the way he thought of me not having my room anymore. When the inside tour ended, we were off to the gardens where I got pictures of Justin. He would ask questions, like did my mommy's grandfather work in these gardens? Was that statue here when you lived here Grammy? Yes, we got a picture of him next to the statue where Doug and I had ours taken. Even the shade garden had grown. A few more hydrangeas and dogwood trees have been added. I used to think that hydrangeas did and still do remind me of snowballs and asked my dad if I could pick them and throw them on the ground and you guessed it- a big No was the answer. A plum tree was planted among the middle of the other trees. Wonder if we would have eaten the plums from the garden? We also got pictures of him next to the camel's hedges. After I moved, Miss Duke brought in two camels. I know many stories have been written of the two new bosses that once roamed the grounds. I have no stories to tell but am sure there are many. The tour person was so nice when talking of them and made a point to show Justin their pictures.

Since the one camel was transferred to New Jersey, and we still live in New Jersey. I am sure one day we can go and see the animal in person but it was fun for us to check out the website of where he is located here in our state at the Popcorn Park.

I am sure there will be more visits in the future, each bringing back memories of sadness and happiness. The first memory would be moving to Rough Point in February of 1961. What was the cottage going to be like? The day I would dread the most, moving away in October of 1968. A day I would not like for a very long time. What was that going to be like? Would Duke Farms be so different from the cottage?

The one item I have, that was my parents bought while we lived at Rough Point, is the end table with the marble top. A few of my mom's items she took to Rough Point from New Jersey when we moved in 1961. A black, music jewelry box with a Japanese lady dancing around, that dad had given me as a surprise. I still miss my two big dolls but I must say they did get good use as I used one of the arms from each doll for a Science Fair Project in high school. My one item I really wanted to come was the canopy bed my dad made. The bed was left in Newport and I often wondered what happened to it.

Friends have asked if I would like to be a tour guide, the answer would be yes, but again I am sure my stories would be of events that I love to tell, not the real history of Rough Point. I do recall in English class when I was a junior I did an oral report on Rough Point. I shared the history of the house, Fredrick Vanderbilt (grandson of Cornelius Vanderbilt) was the first owner of the house and he sold the house to William Leeds. Mr. Duke purchased the home in 1922. I showed pictures of the house, and made a point of showing where the Dukes extended the house. The Ball Room was added on by the Duke Family along with the Solarium and they added on the guest rooms on the second floor. The autograph from the prince who once came to visit and the post card from India Miss Duke sent to my parents. The teacher had no idea I lived there and was quite impressed with the report.

Thinking how did my life change after moving to the summer cottage. I guess I can say it changed in many ways. I met many interesting guests that came to the cottage. When I was a junior in high school and got my license I did get to drive my dad's car. My parents' lives may have changed in some ways. I think one way was the stress might have been taken off, as they had no rent, utilities bills or food to buy. However, I think in some ways now maybe a different kind of stress came upon them. Even with the cost of not paying for food, they did not go overboard with the food we ate. It would be fish sticks or fish chowder on Fridays. Mom would have cake made for us when we came home from school made from scratch, with no frosting or peanut butter cookies that would be cut out from the bottom of a glass that would go great dipped in hot chocolate or a cold glass of milk. I do think they enjoyed living at the cottage and I like to think the cottage became alive when we lived there those short seven and half years. In addition, I must admit now, I am so glad the walls cannot talk. As what would the walls reveal if they could talk, not sure if I really want to know?

One sad note I must say I never did go in the Peace Corp and with thinking back I am not sure how I would have gone knowing how homesick I would get just staying overnight at a friend's house but it was a happy thought way back then.

On a happy note, I did become a citizen of the United States. The year was 1970. My cousin Stella and I took a bus from Springfield to Elizabeth, so all my hard work did not go in vain.

Many years later I did reconnect with my friend Sandy who lived off Vosseler Avenue. Sandy and I would get off the bus at Millers Lane and then we would continue our half hour walk home. I did reconnect with someone from before my move in 1961; we met again in May of 1969. Doug and I were friends when we were little. He was with me when my mom got sick but on the day she died he had to leave to go back to the navy base in California. We married April of 1970, have four children and as of now five grandchildren (Justin, Courtney, Zakk, Madelynn and Olive). I have a snow globe of Rough Point and when I shake it, it reminds me of Heidi trying to find her grandfather. It is my reminder of the past- the happy times and sad times but a time not to forget.

Even after all these years I can still hear my Dad asking "so was Rough Point the big house you always dreamed of living in" and you know it was even with so many of the sad memories. It was a home to me.

Dad in his RCAF uniform

Mom at the front door

Grand staircase

Mr. Duke's bedroom

Ballroom

My parents at Christmas

In the Solarium with my brother and parents

Front lawn with Benny, Mom and Dad with our bow and arrows

Autograph from a Prince from India

Post card from Miss Duke from India

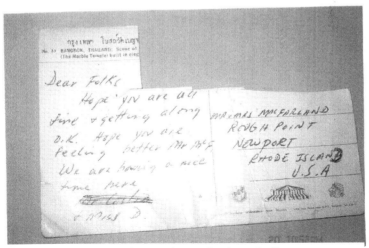

Post card from Miss Duke from India

Bracelet from Mrs. Veary

Cliff Walk with Rough Point at the end

My sister Audrey with her children Lynne and Dawne

My sister Audrey and my niece Dawne

My sister Nita and I with our dogs

My brother Benny with our dog

Second sink in the kitchen

Garden

Front lawn

My dad with the dogs

My dad with the dogs

My dad with the dogs

Family with Mom and Dad in the ballroom

My niece Lynn and I in the kitchen

Last day of school

St. Catherine Academy

Doug and I with Miss Duke's dog in 2000

Justin and I in the garden

Justin in the garden

Madelynn and I with a Rough Point snow globe

My family

December 25, 1967, our last family picture

Rough Point to you,

maybe a summer cottage of a tobacco heiress,

to me, it's a home with many memories.

And so I ask,

What will you take away when visiting?

A Summer Cottage

or

A Little Girl's Memory?

Made in the USA
Columbia, SC
25 August 2017